USURPERS

USURPERS

HOW VOTERS STOPPED THE GOP TAKEOVER OF NORTH CAROLINA'S COURTS

BILLY CORRIHER

ISBN: 978-0-578-91588-3 (print)
       978-0-578-91071-0 (ebook)

billycorriher.com

Cover Design: Dan Almasy
Page layout: Catherine Williams, Chapter One Book Production, UK

Printed in the United States of America

DEDICATION

For my nephews. Stay in school, kids.

TABLE OF CONTENTS

PROLOGUE

The legislature in my home state, North Carolina, passed a bill in 2013 that was literally designed to keep Black voters from casting a ballot. In my job at a progressive think tank in Washington, D.C., I was researching and writing about a provision of the wide-ranging law that flew under the radar but radically changed judicial elections. I didn't know it at the time, but it was the first in a long series of bills that changed how North Carolina's judges were chosen, all of them intended to get judges on the bench who would rubber-stamp voter suppression.

For several years, I worked with organizers and leaders in North Carolina who fought the Republican legislature's attempts to get their preferred judges on the bench. I wrote a series of blog posts to help bring national media attention to the issue. One of them focused on a scheme devised by the 2016 lame-duck legislature to pack the state supreme court, essentially overturning the voters' decision to elect a progressive majority. The GOP was determined to change the courts that were standing in the way of their voter suppression.

The power grabs led to massive protests. In 2014, I drove home and attended a rally for "Moral Monday," the movement led by Rev. William Barber of the North Carolina NAACP that was sweeping across the state. My brother Robert, an organizer, had helped put the event together.

Barber wrote a book in 2016 entitled *The Third Reconstruction*, calling for a movement to counter the country's racial divide. He called on activists to "go home" and "fight in every state capitol."

In 2018, I moved back to North Carolina and worked alongside advocates for voting rights and other democracy reforms. We discussed pending bills with legislators, as Republicans fast-tracked legislation that changed the courts and judicial elections. When the state supreme court heard lawsuits challenging the power grabs, we called out justices for conflicts of interests and asked them to recuse themselves.

I was on the front lines as the legislature tried one last scheme to pack the North Carolina Supreme Court in 2018. Champions of judicial independence fought the scheme in the halls of power, on the campaign trail, and in protests outside the capitol. As politicians attacked the courts, voters and activists rose to their defense.

This book tells the story of that fight. I hope it inspires readers. Lawmakers in other states are engaging in similar power grabs, and this book will shed some light on how to fight them. It's also meant to be a historical record of the legislature's astounding power grabs and brazen attempts at voter suppression. We need to understand how a moderate state like North Carolina ended up with a far-right legislature for more than a decade; how that legislature was opposed; and how its worst power grabs were defeated by voters, activists, and the courts.

THE PLAYERS

THE JUDGES:

- **Cheri Beasley** (D) was chief justice of the North Carolina Supreme Court from 2019 to 2021 and an associate justice from 2012 to 2019. A former public defender, Beasley dissented when the court upheld legislators' racially gerrymandered election districts.

- **Kimberly Best** (D) has served as a judge in Mecklenburg County District Court since 2009. Best spoke out against lawmakers' effort to draw judicial election districts for the county.

- **Roger Gregory** is a judge on the 4th U.S. Circuit Court of Appeals in Richmond, Virginia, which hears appeals from North Carolina. Appointed by President Clinton, Gregory presided over a lawsuit challenging the state's gerrymandered election districts.

- **Bob Hunter** served on the North Carolina Court of Appeals from 2009 to 2014, then again from 2015 to 2019. A moderate Republican, Hunter went back to practicing law after leaving the bench. He represented Best and other Charlotte judges in a racial gerrymandering lawsuit.

- **Diana Gibbons Motz** is a judge on the 4th U.S. Circuit Court of Appeals. She wrote the court's decision to strike down a 2013 voting law for discriminating against Black voters.

- **Paul Newby** (R) has served on the North Carolina Supreme Court since 2005. He wrote the court's 2015 decision to uphold racially gerrymandered election districts.

- **Bob Orr** (R) served on the North Carolina Court of Appeals from 1986 to 1994 and on the North Carolina Supreme Court from 1994 to 2004.

- **James Wynn** is a 4th U.S. Circuit Court of Appeals judge who ruled in cases involving redistricting and the 2013 election law. Confirmed in 2010, Wynn's nomination a decade earlier was blocked by racist Sen. Jesse Helms.

THE LAWYERS:

- **Julius Chambers** was a renowned civil rights attorney based in Charlotte. He brought lawsuits in North Carolina and other states that removed barriers to Black voters gaining political power.

- **Anita Earls** was a civil rights attorney who worked with Chambers before going on to file lawsuits that challenged racial discrimination by the state legislature. She ran for a seat on the North Carolina Supreme Court in 2018, and legislators tried to help her opponent.

- **Robinson Everett** was a Duke law professor and the plaintiff in a racial gerrymandering lawsuit in the 1990s. Everett lived in the 12th congressional district, a serpentine district that stretched across the middle of the state and included several large cities.

- **Thomas Farr** is an election law attorney who represented North Carolina Republicans for several decades. Farr was nominated four times to be a federal judge. Civil rights activists fought his confirmation.

- **Allison Riggs** is a lawyer with the Southern Coalition for Social Justice (SCSJ), an organization founded by Earls. She represented voters in the lawsuit challenging the 2013 voting law and other litigation.

NORTH CAROLINA LEGISLATORS

DEMOCRATS:

- **Sen. Dan Blue** serves as minority leader. From 1991 to 1994, he was speaker of the North Carolina House of Representatives. He is the only Black person to ever hold that role.

- **Gov. Roy Cooper** was elected in 2016. He formerly served in the legislature.

- **Rep. Darren Jackson** was the minority leader from 2017 to 2020. He now serves on the North Carolina Court of Appeals.

- **Sen. Floyd McKissick**, in office from 2007 to 2020, was chair of the Legislative Black Caucus.

- **Rep. Mickey Michaux** served in the North Carolina legislature for decades, from 1973 until his retirement in 2020. Before running for office, Michaux was a civil rights activist.

- **Rep. Marcia Morey**, a former judge, spoke out against laws that targeted the courts.

REPUBLICANS:

- **Sen. Tom Apodaca** helped lead the effort to pass a 2013 voting law that a federal court struck down for discriminating against Black voters.

- **Sen. Phil Berger** has served as president pro tem of the senate since 2010.

- **Rep. Richard Burr** spearheaded an effort to redraw judicial election districts across the state.

- **Rep. David Lewis**, who led the committee in charge of redistricting, announced in 2016 that lawmakers intended to draw congressional districts that would elect 10 Republicans to the state's 13 districts.

- **Rep. Tim Moore** has served as speaker of the House of Representatives since 2015. He has issued statements, co-signed by Berger, criticizing or threatening judges who ruled against the legislature.

- **Gov. Pat McCrory** was elected in 2012 and lost reelection in 2016.

- **Rep. Art Pope** was in the legislature from 1999 to 2003, and after leaving, he used his personal wealth to support Republican candidates and establish conservative media outlets. He served as McCrory's budget director.

- **Sen. Bob Rucho**, in office from 2008 to 2017, played a key role in redistricting.

INTRODUCTION

In the fall of 2020, Americans voted a president out of office in the midst of two things—a deadly pandemic and sustained, widespread social unrest—that the U.S. hadn't seen in generations. Days before the election, President Donald Trump and the Republican Senate rushed to get Amy Coney Barrett confirmed to a seat on the U.S. Supreme Court. Barrett is the third Trump appointee on the Court, which was already a reliable vote in favor of GOP voter suppression.

Voting rights advocates warn that, even with Trump out of office, the judiciary he reshaped still poses a fundamental threat to democracy. Trump and Republican senators created a judicial system that will rubberstamp the GOP's efforts to hang on to power through voter suppression, despite the country's demographic shift.

How did America get to this point? And how do we find our way out?

Some answers could be found in North Carolina, which faced a similar crisis of democracy in the past ten years. For nearly a decade, North Carolina was governed by an all-white Republican cabal that often got fewer votes in legislative races than the other party.

The parallels between Raleigh and D.C. were clear to Rev. William Barber, a national civil rights leader who lives in Eastern

North Carolina. In February 2017, Barber told a crowd of protesters, "We have been preparing all along for such a time as this. The racism and greedy extremism that came to power in North Carolina four years ago now controls the White House and Congress in D.C. ... The whole world is in turmoil, asking what can we do? Well, we know we've got a hard fight ahead. But we know how to win."

The leaders of the North Carolina legislature had shown many of the same autocratic tendencies as Trump: voter suppression, policies that discriminate against people of color, blatant lies, attacking judges as illegitimate, and trying to disregard votes cast by Democrats due to false claims of "voter fraud."

Trump was accused of inciting a deadly insurrection targeting the U.S. Capitol during his final days in office. North Carolina Republicans, by comparison, engaged in slightly more subtle attacks on democracy. In December 2016, Mark Joseph Stern of Slate accused GOP legislators of attempting "an extraordinarily disturbing legislative coup, a flagrant effort to maintain one-party rule by rejecting democratic norms and revoking the will of the voters... It should terrify every American citizen who believes in the rule of law."

A report from the Electoral Integrity Project in 2016 questioned whether North Carolina was still a democracy. A University of North Carolina professor described the state as "a deeply flawed, partly free democracy that is only slightly ahead of the failed democracies that constitute much of the developing world."

In *Strongmen*, author Ruth Ben-Ghiat called Trump an authoritarian, which has traditionally been defined as a president dominating the legislative and judicial branches. In a state like North Carolina, where the governor is a relatively weak chief executive, the legislature has the potential to reign with an iron fist. Historically, the rules of Jim Crow were mostly written by Southern state legislatures, even as segregationist governors got most of the attention.

Both Trump and the North Carolina legislature represented a reaction to changing demographics, the shrinking of the white majority that controlled politics until recent years. They were both backed by powerful corporate interests. And both were determined to pack the courts.

As U.S. Senate Majority Leader Mitch McConnell broke all norms to get Trump's judges on the bench, the North Carolina legislature passed a series of laws and a constitutional amendment to change the courts or manipulate judicial elections. GOP legislators repeatedly threatened judges who ruled against them.

The Republicans in Raleigh invented new power grabs in their attempts to get GOP judges on the bench. But most of their schemes were thwarted by voters or the courts. Activists and lawyers fought these power grabs, the media sounded the alarm, and voters elected judges who restored democracy.

Part I of this book documents some of the courtroom battles over voter suppression in North Carolina and introduces the lawyers representing voters and the GOP legislature. It also documents the beginning of the Moral Monday movement to resist the legislature's power grabs.

Part II focuses on the battles over the courts themselves, as Republicans in Raleigh and Washington, D.C. tried to install judges that would rubber stamp voter suppression.

The conclusion, Part III, focuses on the ramifications of voters and activists defeating the legislature's worst power grabs. The voters protected judicial independence, and the courts found a way to restore checks and balances and protect the rights of voters.

This story began in 2010, when Republicans won control of both houses of the North Carolina legislature for the first time in a century. They drew election districts that helped their party's candidates by packing Democratic voters into a handful of districts, and their all-white caucus grew larger. In 2013, the legislature passed a voter ID law that was designed to keep African Americans from casting a ballot. Their gerrymandered election districts gave them enough votes to override the governor's veto. The GOP kept its majority, even when the other party got more total votes.

The only check on their power was the courts. Civil rights lawyer Anita Earls took the legislature to court—state and federal—for discriminating against Black voters in their voter ID law and their election districts. She laid out the undeniable evidence of racial discrimination. And the legislature's attorney, Thomas Farr, repeatedly tried to justify the legislature's actions as attempts to comply with the Voting Rights Act of 1965 (VRA).

Earls and Farr argued before Black federal judges whose nominations had been blocked for years by racist Republican Sen. Jesse Helms, a former client of Farr's. The federal courts protected voting rights by striking down the voter ID law and the racially gerrymandered election districts.

Farr won twice at the North Carolina Supreme Court, as the conservative majority accepted lawmakers' claims that packing Black voters into majority-Black election districts was a good-faith effort to comply with the VRA. The Republican State Leadership Committee (RSLC), which had funded the GOP's 2010 takeover and helped gerrymander the districts, had spent big in the 2012 election to keep the court's conservative majority in place.

The U.S. Supreme Court, however, overturned the state supreme court's decisions and forced lawmakers to redraw the districts. Republican politicians like Rep. David Lewis, a tall tobacco farmer, attacked judges who ruled against them and accused them of "legislating from the bench." When lawmakers redrew the districts, Lewis stated clearly that the new districts would discriminate against Democratic voters and help Republicans.

To keep the courts from blocking their power grabs, legislators tried to control the judicial branch. A 2013 memo from GOP consultant John Davis had advised legislators that "supreme court races are critical for long-term Republican dominance. Lose the courts, lose the war." According to NC Policy Watch, the memo was titled, "How the North Carolina Republican Party can maintain political power for 114 years." Davis noted that the GOP majority could "initiate radical reforms," and Republicans spent the next several years trying to reshape the courts.

Never before had a legislature proposed so many sweeping changes to how judges are chosen. Republicans tried to cancel the 2016 North Carolina Supreme Court election. When that failed and the voters elected a progressive majority, they briefly considered a proposal to pack the court and essentially overturn the results. Instead, legislators passed bills giving themselves more power over the courts and the executive branch (after voters elected a Democratic governor).

Legislators also passed bills that gerrymandered judges, un-packed the court of appeals, and manipulated election ballots to help Republican judicial candidates.

The state courts blocked some of these laws, and they kept the legislature from putting its allies in charge of running elections. They ruled that these power grabs violated the state constitution, which meant that federal courts couldn't overturn the decisions.

In the summer of 2018, Republican lawmakers passed a constitutional amendment that would give themselves control over filling vacant judicial seats. It would've opened the door to another court-packing scheme.

Around the same time, Republicans in Washington, D.C., were pushing to nominate Farr to a federal court in Eastern North Carolina, where around half of the population is Black. Barber and other activists around the country raised concerns about Farr's history of defending discrimination and his ties to a white-supremacist lawyer.

Activists, judges, and so many others stood up against Republicans' push for judges who would rubber stamp their voter suppression. The Moral Monday movement, headed by Barber, rallied thousands at the state capitol to protest the power grabs. Activists toured the state to educate voters on the importance of independent courts.

In 2017, after Trump's election had ensured that voters could no longer count on federal courts, Earls decided to run for a seat on the state supreme court. It was a challenge for a quiet, reserved lawyer who was more at home in the courtroom than on the campaign trail. Earls campaigned on a platform of judicial independence, as the legislature passed laws intended to hurt her campaign.

On Election Day in 2018, voters rejected the legislature's court-packing amendment and elected Earls to the high court, defying the GOP's effort to support the incumbent. Now, Earls serves on a court with the power to block unconstitutional state laws. During her first year in office, state courts halted a discriminatory voter ID law, expanded voting rights for people with felony convictions, and ordered legislators to redraw election districts that were blatantly gerrymandered in favor of Republicans.

This year, the courts will likely have the chance to review new election districts based on the 2020 census. Judges have the precedents they need to ensure that the districts aren't so biased that they determine which party should govern.

Other states aren't so lucky. The North Carolina legislature's power grabs have become a playbook for gerrymandered Republican legislatures facing Democratic governors or high courts. And given the current ideology of the U.S. Supreme Court, these state courts are crucial to protecting individual rights and safeguarding democracy. They're the best chance to stop partisan gerrymandering and discriminatory, unfair voting laws.

PART I

THE BATTLE IN THE COURTS

CHAPTER 1

RED MAP

Republicans in Washington, D.C. planned to spend millions of dollars on state legislative elections in 2010. Their goal was to control the redrawing of election districts after the Census. The new districts would keep their party in power, regardless of what the voters wanted. Their districts would also lead to drawn out legal battles across the country. North Carolina, in particular, saw dozens of lawsuits over unfair election districts.

The GOP's 2010 strategy was spearheaded by the Republican State Leadership Committee (RSLC), a group funded by some of the largest corporations in the U.S. The RSLC's mission was to elect GOP state legislators, and the group's REDMAP project would then help these legislators gerrymander election districts. GOP strategist Karl Rove, an architect of the plan, said that "when you draw the lines, you make the rules." Critics warned that Republicans sought to create a "permanent majority" in Congress.

Chris Jankowski founded the RSLC in 2002, and he claimed much of the credit for REDMAP's success. In *Ratf**ked*, Dave Daley's history of the post-2010 gerrymanders, Jankowski said that he targeted states that were likely to gain or lose congressional seats and states where control of the legislature was up for grabs.

Rove helped develop the idea and pitched it to corporate donors. The RSLC received millions of dollars from special interests like the U.S. Chamber of Commerce and American Justice Partnership, a group linked to the American Legislative Exchange Council (ALEC). The group also received large contributions from Big Tobacco, Wal-mart, and dark money groups that don't disclose their donors.

Jankowski said the RSLC had gone beyond "selling access." He told Daley, "We were selling an outcome and an impact on the political system." By Labor Day 2010, the group had raised three times more than its counterpart, the Democratic Legislative Campaign Committee.

The GOP gained 680 total legislative seats in the midterm elections, the largest sweep in 50 years. They completely controlled redistricting in swing states like North Carolina, Ohio, Pennsylvania, and Wisconsin.

The RSLC worked with local Republican funders. In North Carolina, they partnered with campaign donor Art Pope to fund the takeover of the state legislature. Pope, a discount retail mogul, used his wealth to fund conservative think tanks and help Republican candidates. Pope was the largest political donor in the state.

In Jane Meyer's 2011 profile, she described Pope's philosophy: "Pope believes that wealth is the just reward for talent and hard work, and that all Americans have a fair chance at success." A former Republican legislator, Pope created a network of think tanks and political groups, including some linked to the billionaire Koch brothers, to push his anti-government philosophy. Meyer said Pope had "created a singular influence machine that, according to critics, blurs the lines between tax-deductible philanthropy and corporate-funded partisan advocacy."

The Pope family has spent tens of millions of dollars to influence elections in North Carolina. This money has helped push state politics to the right. With the RSLC's backing in 2010, the Pope groups and other independent spenders shelled out $3 million, a five-fold increase from the last election. And 90 percent of that money helped Republicans, according to an analysis by Facing South, an online magazine by the Institute for Southern Studies in Durham.

Pope's secret-money group, Real Jobs NC, spent millions of dollars, after a seven-figure donation from the RSLC. And in 18 of the 22 elections targeted by the group, the Republican candidate won.

Earlier that year, the U.S. Supreme Court had issued its decision in *Citizens United*, which led to unfettered donations to and spending by independent groups. North Carolina Republicans benefited from campaign ads run by the Koch brothers' Americans for Prosperity and Civitas Action, a local secret-money group linked to Pope.

In North Carolina, some of this money funded ads attacking Democratic legislators who had supported the Racial Justice Act, a bill that sought to prevent executions of people on death row if race played a part in their cases. The legislation was a response to widespread discrimination in the criminal justice system and decades of inaction by the courts, but conservatives used it as fodder for racially tinged attack ads.

Republicans in 2010 won control of the North Carolina legislature for the first time in more than a century, and the GOP caucus was all white.

The last time Republicans controlled the legislature, the state had been in the midst of the post-Civil War Reconstruction. The GOP, then the party of newly enfranchised Black voters, had its ascendancy halted by racist Democrats who established Jim Crow. When Republicans banded together with poor white farmers on a "fusion" platform, Democrats had used violence and demagoguery to stay in power. They had also gerrymandered the heavily Black

Northeastern part of the state.

The history of Democratic power grabs meant that the GOP that finally won power in 2010 had a long list of grievances. When North Carolina elected Republican governors and lieutenant governors in the 1970s and 1980s, Democratic legislators had responded by chipping away at executive power and transferring some of that authority to their own branch. One such law created a commission, appointed entirely by the legislature, to review state agency regulations. Another bill converted some agency officials from political appointees to career civil servants, keeping Democratic appointees in charge.

When Democrats were in control, Republicans had argued that election districts should be drawn by an independent commission to keep districts fair for both parties. Former House Minority Leader Rep. Darren Jackson, now an appellate court judge, acknowledged the reversal by both parties. He said that when the Democrats found themselves in the minority, "the first thing we said was, 'Hey, how about independent redistricting?' And the first thing Republicans said was, 'How about epic payback?'"

Republicans packed Black voters, who overwhelmingly vote Democratic, into certain districts. The population of North Carolina is 60 percent white, but the state is rapidly diversifying, which spelled long-term trouble for the GOP.

Legislators argued they created majority-Black districts to comply with the Voting Rights Act. In a series of cases out of North Carolina, the federal courts had balanced the need for districts that didn't disadvantage Black voters with the Constitution's prohibition on race-based decision making. North Carolina legislators threw off that balance in 2011.

Rev. Barber and many others described the legislature's gerrymandered districts as a form of voter suppression, the latest attempt to keep Black people from exercising political power. Through the next three elections, Republicans maintained a legislative supermajority large enough to overturn any vetoes by the governor. The GOP only won a slim majority of the total votes, but the skewed election districts gave them a supermajority.

The same was true in Wisconsin, Ohio, and other gerrymandered swing states. In some elections, Republicans maintained control even when they received fewer votes.

In North Carolina, the new districts would make it nearly impossible for Democrats to win a majority in the legislature. Conservative commentator John Hood predicted, "GOP candidates could win just over half of the statewide vote for Congress and end up with 62 percent to 77 percent of the seats." And in 2012, more than half of North Carolina voters chose Democratic candidates for Congress, but Republicans won 10 out of 13 seats.

The districts for legislative elections also favored the GOP, which maintained a supermajority with around half the votes. This extreme gerrymandering meant that legislators weren't accountable to voters. They didn't have to worry about whether they'd lose their seats on Election Day.

To justify this unfairness, GOP leaders pointed to gerrymanders by previous Democratic majorities. But technological advances allowed legislators in 2011 to draw maps that benefited their party to a much greater degree than previous maps. A 2014 analysis, using a new tool to measure the extent of partisan gerrymandering, found that the election districts in North Carolina and many other states were "the most extreme gerrymanders in modern history."

Legislators can feel free to ignore the concerns of communities that have been gerrymandered. Eric Holder, the first Black U.S. Attorney General and founder of the National Democratic Redistricting Committee, said, "It is not a coincidence that you see the greatest amount of voter suppression in those states where you see the greatest amount of gerrymandering." Rev. Barber said, "They would not have the power to do what they're doing without racist voter suppression and racist gerrymandering."

North Carolina's Republican legislators could do whatever they wanted. They could pass bills that were unpopular or harmful, without worrying about losing their majority. In 2013, they even passed a voter suppression bill that echoed Jim Crow legislation.

But lawmakers didn't count on civil rights lawyer Anita Earls, a relentless advocate for voters. In the coming years, she would stand before dozens of judges and—in a controlled but urgent tone—systematically dismantle the legislature's justifications for gerrymandering and voter suppression.

Over and over again, Earls and her organization would fight for North Carolina voters. When a federal court blocked the legislature's 2013 voter suppression law, Earls said the court had made clear that legislators "can't discriminate against voters because of their race, and I think that you can't put in place a whole host of measures all at once all with the impact of making it hard to vote." Observers were shocked at the judges' finding that legislators had intentionally targeted Black voters. Earls told a reporter, "Nobody thought it could happen."

CHAPTER 2

JUSTICE ELUDED THEM

Anita Earls was born in 1960, on the eve of the country's civil rights revolution, and she witnessed racial discrimination at a young age. She felt a calling to help people in her community get justice. This led her to a career in civil rights law, defending people from discrimination and disenfranchisement.

Earls was adopted from a foster home as a baby. She was raised by a Black father and white mother, who had moved to Seattle because they couldn't legally marry in the state where they met. Her biological parents had also been an interracial couple, and the controversy had led them to put her up for adoption. Earls' adoptive parents both worked in healthcare, and in a recent interview, she recalled seeing them struggle to make ends meet.

Her dad was a urological technician, but as a Black worker who lacked formal education, he wasn't paid as much as his colleagues. Earls said, "My mom and dad would have to decide what bills to pay and what not to pay." She recalled being told not to answer the phone, in case it was bill collectors calling.

When Earls was six years old, her family integrated an all-white neighborhood in Seattle. Some of her neighbors made sure her family felt unwelcome. One neighbor would "turn her garden hose on us, if we rode our bikes on the sidewalk in front of her house."

Earls' brother was once chased out of a friend's house, a gate striking his back as it was slammed shut. Her brother was bleeding. Her father was furious. Earls' father fumed as he walked over to confront the white family and tell them they couldn't hurt his kids. "I was terrified that something was going to happen to my dad," Earls recalled.

Growing up biracial in the 1960s, Earls was aware at a young age that people in her family and community needed help. She saw that "justice eluded them."

Earls decided in middle school that she wanted to be a lawyer. "I wanted to be a voice for people that didn't have a voice." She also felt a "responsibility to bring together my family, my community and my country across the racial lines that divided us. Indeed, I saw that my life, my very survival depended on it," Earls said in 2019.

Her family couldn't pay for college, but Earls received scholarships to attend Williams College, a small liberal arts school in the Northwest corner of Massachusetts. She went on to attend Yale Law School, with plans to become an advocate for racial justice.

Earls graduated in 1988 and went to work for a law firm founded by renowned civil rights lawyer Julius Chambers, who had won redistricting lawsuits that helped elect the first Black members of Congress from North Carolina in nearly 100 years.

In 1982, Congress had reauthorized the Voting Rights Act (VRA) and clarified that it applied to election laws or practices that impacted voters of color more than others, not just laws that were explicitly meant to disenfranchise people. Chambers and other civil rights lawyers then brought lawsuits challenging election systems that had kept candidates supported by Black voters out of office.

Chambers filed a lawsuit challenging North Carolina's legislative election districts, which included urban counties with multi-member districts in which a few candidates were elected countywide, instead of in individual districts. This system had kept Black voters in these cities from exercising political power in the legislature. The U.S. Supreme Court unanimously agreed with Chambers and struck down the districts.

In the *Gingles* ruling, the Court laid out how judges should decide when a state's election districts violate the VRA by "diluting" the power of voters of color. The group of voters must be large but compact enough to make up a majority in a district, and there must be some degree of racially polarized voting in which white and Black voters choose different candidates. If those conditions were met, lawmakers couldn't deprive Black voters of political power by dividing their community into several districts.

Soon after Earls joined Chambers' old firm, she met the legendary civil rights attorney, who was then director of the NAACP Legal Defense and Education Fund. "He would come by the law firm whenever he was in Charlotte, visiting his family," she said. Earls would get nervous as Chambers made the rounds, asking the young lawyers about their cases. She was thinking, "How am I going to impress this civil rights giant with the little cases I'm working on?"

Earls became a civil rights lawyer at a time when courts were becoming more conservative and more willing to limit the reach of anti-discrimination laws. The courthouse doors were "increasingly being closed to the claims of the people in the communities that I wanted to represent," she said. In Ari Berman's *Give Us the Ballot*, he argued that Republicans in the Reagan administration had begun implementing their anti-civil rights agenda by "changing the courts."

Earls wrote a piece for *The Nation* describing how she spent her early career trying to convince federal courts "that it was important to protect minority voting rights. I found myself defending, again and again … some of the gains Julius Chambers achieved."

She worked at the Department of Justice in the late 1990s, helping state legislators prepare for redistricting in 2000.

While working for The Advancement Project in Washington, D.C., Earls traveled to Florida for a voting rights case related to the disputed 2000 election. She was inspired by the work that local litigators were doing on the ground. "We weren't having that kind of impact," in terms of breaking down barriers to political participation, she said. "We just weren't as close to the voters."

In 2007, Earls returned to North Carolina and founded the Southern Coalition for Social Justice (SCSJ) in Durham. The group's goal was to empower communities to dismantle structural racism and oppression. She secured funding for a new regional organization dedicated to "community lawyering," a collaborative model that seeks to foster grassroots leadership.

SCSJ started with a series of listening tours around the state, asking people what they needed. "We tried to fill in the gaps," Earls said. After hearing from the communities they wanted to help, SCSJ's lawyers took on cases involving criminal justice, the environment, and voting rights. "Those issues were at the top of the list for so many communities in our state, and they weren't getting enough attention," she said.

Earls litigated many of SCSJ's voting rights cases. "What's uniform across the South is that Republicans are using race as a central basis in drawing districts for partisan advantage," she said in an interview with Ari Berman.

In 2013, as Earls' long trials challenging the Republican legislature were just beginning, Chambers passed away. In an interview with WUNC in Durham, Earls discussed his legacy and how much Chambers cared about the lives of "ordinary people." She said, "He cared about them having an equal opportunity and justice, and that's what guides and sustains me."

In the early 1990s, Earls had gotten the chance to work alongside Chambers on a case that made it to the U.S. Supreme

Court. "I learned a tremendous amount from him," she said. The two lawyers were defending election districts that had been redrawn by the Democratic-led North Carolina legislature, after Republican U.S. Attorney General Bill Barr had asked for a second majority-Black Congressional district.

CHAPTER 3

MAJORITY MINORITY

A Democratic legislature in 1991 drew a majority-Black election district that sprawled across the middle of North Carolina, reaching out to encompass the state's largest cities. Republican attorney Thomas Farr filed two lawsuits challenging the districts, and Earls defended the legislature. The U.S. Supreme Court would ultimately side with Farr and describe the districts as "political apartheid." Ten years later, Farr would rack up another victory over a Democratic legislature, this time in state court.

After the 1990 Census, North Carolina gained a seat in Congress, and a coalition of unusual bedfellows—Republicans and Black Democrats—were pushing the legislature to draw a second majority-minority district, which means that people of color are a majority of the voting-age population. In a letter to legislators in 1991, the U.S. Department of Justice said that without that district, it wouldn't approve the districts under the VRA, which required states with a history of voting discrimination to "preclear" voting laws with the federal government.

In the basement of the legislature, lawyer Gerry Cohen drew new Congressional districts. He had drawn the districts in the

1980s with colored pencils and Magic Markers. This time, the legislature provided a computer that could process demographic data. The district Cohen drew wasn't exactly what Republicans had in mind.

The GOP hoped that a second majority-minority district would help them win seats in neighboring districts. Republican lawyer Bob Hunter, who would later become a judge in North Carolina, worked as a consultant for the U.S. Department of Justice, advising state legislators on redistricting. He advocated in court for more majority-minority districts, which he also argued would make Republican candidates competitive in other districts.

As Berman noted in *Give Us the Ballot*, Republicans wanted "to form an improbable partnership with Black Democrats in the South to overthrow the white Democrats who had controlled the region since the end of Reconstruction."

Some Black Democrats in North Carolina, including Rev. Thomas Walker, concluded, "We have to look out for our interests first and the party second." The state chapters of the ACLU and NAACP signed on to the idea of a second majority-Black district.

But not every Black Democrat was on board. Rep. Toby Fitch argued that Republicans were motivated by partisanship, not out of concern for the VRA. Sen. Dan Blue accused Republicans of trying to "corrupt the Voting Rights Act to the extent they can … use it for political advantage."

The Department of Justice's letter to the legislature discussed a potential second majority-minority district that stretched along the state's Southern border, from Charlotte to the coastal city of Wilmington. This district would allow for Black and Native American[1] voting power, since it included much of the Lumbee Tribe. Drawing this district was expected to weaken white Democrats in Eastern North Carolina.

---

1   Many Lumbee prefer the term "American Indian." Malinda Maynor Lowery, *The Lumbee Indians: An American Struggle* (Chapel Hill, North Carolina: The University of North Carolina Press, 2018), 11.

Instead of the GOP's proposed district, Cohen drew a majority-Black district that encompassed most of the state's big cities, stretching 150 miles from Charlotte to Durham, along Interstate 85. Cohen's map managed to preserve power for both Democratic politicians and Black voters.

Republicans were outraged. They pointed out that Democrats had gerrymandered the districts to protect their own political power. Pope, who was then a Republican legislator, filed a partisan gerrymandering lawsuit. He was represented by Farr and his partner Tom Ellis, both of whom who had represented U.S. Sen. Jesse Helms when he was accused of intimidating Black voters with misleading postcards. Ellis had been a political adviser to Helms, and he was Farr's mentor.

The lawsuit filed by Ellis and Farr pointed out that much of the new majority-Black District was no wider than Interstate 85. They said Democratic legislators had divided towns and counties into two or three districts. Pope's lawsuit also noted that the Democratic majority had rejected more compact maps that Republicans had offered, as well as maps drawn by nonpartisan, good-government groups.

During oral arguments, Farr argued that the shape of the districts themselves—with the new 12th district sprawling diagonally across the middle of the state—was enough evidence of gerrymandering to take the case to trial. But the case was thrown out, with the judges noting that the U.S. Supreme Court had "consistently accepted the view that redistricting is an inherently political process."

After their loss, Farr and his clients sought to join a racial gerrymandering lawsuit filed by Robinson Everett, a professor at Duke law school. A white Democrat, Everett was within the Northern stretch of the 12th District, which was represented in Congress by Mel Watt, a Black Democrat and former partner at Chambers' law firm. The NAACP and its allies responded to the suit by pointing out that "white voters have no constitutionally protectible right to vote in a majority-white district."

Everett argued for a "color blind" vision of the Constitution, which means that the government shouldn't take race into consideration for any of its decisions, including redistricting. Theodore Johnson of the Brennan Center for Justice recently described this vision of the Constitution as "protecting white Americans from the discrimination that some conservatives perceive results from attempts to remediate historical wrongs."

As described in Tinsley Yarbrough's *Race and Redistricting,* Farr argued at trial that the legislature hadn't bothered to ask whether the goal of ensuring Black political power required districts that were more than 50 percent Black. He also cross-examined Rep. Fitch about previous statements criticizing GOP proposals for two majority-Black districts. Fitch's answer was that the Republicans' earlier proposals weren't actually "intended to help minorities."

Defending the legislature, Earls argued that the districts complied with the Constitution and the VRA. An experienced appellate lawyer, Chambers was brought onto the defense team after the U.S. Supreme Court took the case.

Earls said that Chambers had an ability to predict the other side's argument that she lacked as a young lawyer. When they were having dinner the night before oral arguments, she was surprised to hear Chambers predict that the other side would compare the state's majority-minority districts to "whites only" signs on water fountains.

The oral arguments at the Court the next day focused on the unusual, serpentine shape of the district. Justice Sandra Day O'Connor asked in her Texas drawl whether "a district such as this could be in and of itself some evidence of an invidious intent?"

Later that year, O'Connor wrote the court's decision in favor of Farr's clients. The vote was 5-4, with five Republican appointees in the majority. The opinion called the map "so irrational on its face that it can be understood only as an effort to segregate voters into separate voting districts because of their race."

The conservative majority said the misshapen district "reinforces the perception that members of the same racial group—regardless of their age, education, economic status, or the community in which they live—think alike, share the same political interests, and will prefer the same candidates at the polls. We have rejected such perceptions elsewhere as impermissible racial stereotypes."

Chambers had warned Earls that the districts would be compared to Jim Crow segregation, and the Court's opinion said that they bore "an uncomfortable resemblance to political apartheid."

In dissent, Justice Byron White argued that it "strained credulity" to suggest that the mostly white state legislature drew the districts for the purpose of discriminating against white voters. But the majority sidestepped this issue. The Court's ruling was criticized for failing to give legislators clarity. Hunter, the Republican lawyer, described the ruling as "just crazy."

Reflecting on the case decades later, Earls believes they lost "because it was a 51 percent Black district." In cases brought by Chambers, the courts had specified when majority-minority districts were justified. Much of the credit for the GOP's win went to Farr.

The case was sent back to the lower court, and the map was redrawn. The general location of the two majority-Black districts remained the same, though the 12th district became shorter and more compact. The redrawn district, with a substantial Black minority, was upheld in 2001 by the U.S. Supreme Court, which ruled that partisanship, not race, was the legislature's motive for drawing the district.

In 2002, Farr filed a lawsuit in state court challenging Democrats' new legislative election districts. He was looking to persuade the North Carolina Supreme Court, which had a GOP majority, to rule that Democrats' legislative election districts violated a long-dormant amendment to the state constitution.

North Carolina voters in 1968 approved an amendment that banned the dividing of counties when drawing legislative election districts. Before the VRA was passed in 1965, "multi-member" election districts had served to keep Black voters from being a majority in urban districts. The 1968 amendment meant that North Carolina legislators would continue to use multiple, countywide election districts for large, urban counties. This could dilute the political power of Black voters, as Earls and others have pointed out.

Legislators enforced the amendment in the 1970s, even though it hadn't been submitted to the the federal government for pre-clearance, as the VRA required for states with a history of voting discrimination. In the early 1980s, when the state finally requested preclearance, the Department of Justice concluded that requiring multi-member districts conflicted with the VRA. This led the legislature to stop enforcing the amendment.

In 2002, however, Farr's lawsuit argued that the amendment should be enforced to the extent possible under federal law. He wanted the state supreme court to strike down the Democrats' new districts for violating the amendment. Farr noted that the Department of Justice's objection letter said that it shouldn't "be regarded as precluding the state from following a policy of preserving county lines whenever feasible in formulating new districts."

In April 2002, the court's Republican majority breathed new life into the amendment. In *Stephenson v. Bartlett*, the court interpreted the Department of Justice's objection as a prohibition on multi-member districts, not an objection to the amendment itself. And it said the amendment's goals could be preserved, without violating federal law.

The court laid out a new process, unique to North Carolina, that legislators must follow to reconcile the whole county amendment and the VRA. Legislators would start by drawing the districts required by the VRA, while complying with the amendment as much as possible. Then, they would implement the amendment for the rest of the districts. For counties large enough for multiple districts, all the districts would be within the county. Smaller counties would be combined into clusters, for some reason, and the clusters would be divided into districts.

The two Democratic justices dissented and argued the "whole county" amendment was unconstitutional. Justice G.K. Butterfield, a Black Democrat who now serves in Congress, wrote a powerful dissent. "My view of the people's intent does not include the sacred nostalgia for whole counties that the majority seems to embrace," he said. The previous electoral system, which was preserved by the amendment, had resulted in an all-white state legislature.

Butterfield denied that the 1968 amendment "represented the will of all of the people." He said the electorate failed to include Black people who were legally eligible to vote but blocked from registering. (Two years after the 1968 amendment, voters had declined to repeal the constitutional literacy test for voting.)

After the *Stephenson* decision, the legislature redrew the districts. And for the next decade, election districts seemed relatively fair. Each party's portion of the votes roughly translated to a similar portion of legislative seats.

In 2010, Republicans won big in these districts, giving them a majority in the legislature. When this new majority drew their own election districts, Earls said that "they just totally violated" the whole county amendment. Legislators sliced through counties in their efforts to disenfranchise voters who didn't support their party.

In the coming years, Earls and Farr would become familiar foes, representing opposing sides in cases involving redistricting and voter suppression in North Carolina. Earls would represent voters who were gerrymandered or disenfranchised by the GOP legislature.

Farr would, again and again, defend Republicans accused of discrimination. He had spent his early career suing the long-ruling Democrats, but after the GOP took power, he found himself defending a new establishment.

The attorney was nominated to be a federal judge by President George W. Bush, but his confirmation didn't move forward. Among other things, civil rights groups raised questions about his relationship to Ellis, who was a white supremacist. Ellis had been a leader of the Pioneer Fund, which supported research into the genetic superiority of white people.

Farr had helped Ellis and Sen. Helms create a network of groups to fund right-wing causes. In 2007, after his nomination stalled, Farr gave a speech honoring Ellis. The occasion was Ellis receiving an award from Hillsdale College, Farr's alma mater and a conservative college that still forgoes federal funding to avoid complying with civil rights laws.

President Bush failed to get Farr on the bench. But years later, Republicans would try again.

CHAPTER 4

TURNING A BLIND EYE TO RACIAL GERRY-MANDERING

In January 2014, Farr and Earls met at the North Carolina Supreme Court in downtown Raleigh. They argued over whether Republicans had gerrymandered Black voters when they drew election districts a few years earlier. Like the U.S. Supreme Court two decades earlier, the justices would side with Farr.

The high court hears cases in a building on Morgan Street, across from the historical capitol building that until 2020 was surrounded by several monuments—including a 75-foot-tall obelisk—honoring Confederate soldiers and leaders. The words "LAW AND JUSTICE" adorn the top of the building's facade, just below a granite sculpture of a robed man with a flowing beard, holding on to a bundle of scrolls. The U.S. and North Carolina flags fly above him.

The courtroom is on the third floor, the double doors opening to rows of black chairs for spectators, behind tables for the two opposing parties. The dark wooden walls are lined by subtle, square semi-columns. Except for one wall with tall windows, the courtroom is surrounded by portraits of former chief justices. Almost all of them are white men.

The chief justice sits in the middle of the seven adjudicators, who look slightly down from behind their long table when court is in session. Until December 2020, a massive portrait of former Chief Justice Thomas Ruffin, three times larger than the others, loomed behind the middle seat. Ruffin was pictured standing in a suit, his hand gripping a book on a desk. His white hair and white shirt framed his long, stern face.

Ruffin, a slaveowner who brutalized and raped enslaved people, had been appointed to the state supreme court by the antebellum state legislature in 1829. He was in power for decades. In decisions he wrote, the court sanctioned brutality by other enslavers. He wrote the opinion when the court unanimously overturned a small fine imposed on a man who shot an enslaved woman whom he had rented. Ruffin wrote that an enslaved person must know "that there is no appeal from his master."

After the post-Civil War Reconstruction, racist white Democrats like Ruffin had used violence and voter suppression to take control of the state government, including the courts. They ruled for a century. North Carolina, like other Southern states, was a one-party state. There were no Republicans on the state supreme court from 1896 to 1994, though the Democrats were from the party's right and left wings.

By the 1990s, the parties had begun to more clearly sort into two different ideologies, and judicial elections were getting more politicized and competitive. In 1994, voters elected two Republican justices, including Judge Bob Orr. In 1998, Republicans gained a majority, and after the 2002 election, only one Democrat remained. (After this election, the legislature switched to nonpartisan judicial elections.)

The North Carolina Supreme Court still included a conservative majority in January 2014, when Earls found herself arguing before the justices that the legislature's 2011 election districts were unconstitutional. She thought the voters had a good chance. "The state constitutional claims were so strong," she reflected in a recent interview.

Before the court convened, Earls sat at her party's table, hunched over documents. Other lawyers were mingling and chatting with observers behind her. She would occasionally scribble notes on a yellow pad.

The bailiff asked everyone to silence their cell phones and explained the schedule for the day. Earls organized her documents and waited. A few minutes later, the gavel banged, and a bailiff announced, "The honorable, the chief justices and the associate justices." Everyone stood as the justices entered. "God save the state and this honorable court."

The court's Democratic chief justice, who would soon reach the mandatory retirement age, sat in front of Ruffin's massive portrait and announced the first case. Earls stood and shifted over to the podium. With a map of a Raleigh election district propped up behind her, she attacked the trial court's ruling to uphold the districts. Earls described the VRA justification as "a remedy imposed against the wishes of the very votes they were allegedly intended to benefit."

She suggested the districts would undermine "decades of progress toward what all of us want, a political process in which candidates are judged not on the color of their skin, but the content of their character."

Representing voting rights advocates and an interracial group of voters, Earls employed the language of judges who believed in a "color blind" constitution. "The imposition of racial quotas in these redistricting maps, even with a benign purpose, was the most constitutionally objectionable use of race possible." She said the fundamental issue was that, before these maps, Black candidates had won in legislative districts that weren't majority-Black. Earls quoted Justice O'Connor's warning about "political apartheid."

Earls laid out the process by which Republicans had sought a map that included a percentage of majority-Black districts that roughly matched the state's Black population. They didn't take the time to ask whether majority-Black districts were actually necessary to avoid disenfranchising Black voters, as the VRA requires.

Pointing to the map of the Raleigh district, Earls noted that the new majority-Black district was represented by Senate Minority Leader Dan Blue, a Black Democrat who had been overwhelmingly elected in the previous, majority-white district. "White voters voted for Dan Blue," she said, "There was no need for this remedy."

At that point, almost 15 minutes in, Republican Justice Mark Martin asked the first question, which was about a prior racial gerrymandering ruling. Martin said it's a "complex area of the law" and asked how much deference is usually awarded to legislatures.

Earls said that, contrary to the trial court's ruling, there was no "leeway" when reconciling the VRA and constitutional bans on racial discrimination. Courts had rejected arguments that majority-Black districts were a "safe harbor" defense to racial gerrymandering claims.

In conclusion, Earls asked the court to order new districts. "Voters know when their neighborhoods are being divided along racial lines," she said. Racially polarized voting was declining in North Carolina. "To resegregate voters … in these kinds of districts, it is a step backward," she concluded.

She gathered her documents and sat down. Earls recalled years later that the justices had been "extremely quiet" during her argument and it was "very hard to tell where they might end up."

Her co-counsel, Eddie Speas representing the Democratic Party, then rose and argued that the legislature had violated the "whole county" provision of the state constitution. Speas argued legislators had violated the "plain text" of the 2002 *Stephenson* decision, which outlined how they can comply with both the VRA and whole county provision. (*See previous chapter.*)

Farr then stood to defend the districts. He started with a joke about how he and the justices keep "meeting this way." Farr argued that legislators had leeway to draw majority-minority districts to "protect the state" from potential lawsuits under the VRA. He leaned on the podium and laid out why he thought majority-Black districts were justified. Farr described the persistence of racially polarized voting.

Martin asked the attorney how courts should deal with the fact that the districts will impact "political outcomes." Farr smiled and stood up straight. "It's not something the court *can* assess," he said. The U.S. Supreme Court had made it nearly impossible for federal judges to strike down districts for being too biased towards one party. Legislators acknowledged that the districts favored the GOP, Farr said, but that's not what the case was about.

In December 2014, nearly a year after the arguments, the North Carolina Supreme Court upheld the districts. The conservative majority said the legislature's "desire to comply with the Voting Rights Act is justifiable."

In dissent, Justice Cheri Beasley noted that the VRA requires map-drawers to consider the "totality of circumstances," instead of drawing districts with an arbitrary percentage of Black voters. She cited rulings by the U.S. Supreme Court, which had just ruled in a racial gerrymandering lawsuit out of Alabama. Lawmakers there had argued that the VRA justified districts that were overwhelmingly Black. But the justices had rejected the Alabama legislature's justification.

Beasley criticized the majority for not sending the case back to the trial court, which all of the justices agreed had applied the wrong legal standard. She warned that the court's departure from its "settled principles of appellate review could create a stain of suspicion among the citizens of the state regarding the actions of their elected officials and bodies of government—both legislative and judicial."

The plaintiffs appealed to the U.S. Supreme Court, which ordered the justices in Raleigh to take another look. But in 2015, the state supreme court upheld the districts again. The justices voted along ideological lines, though the conservative majority had shrunk to 4-3 after the previous year's election.

The decision, written by conservative Justice Paul Newby, said the legislature had "identified past or present discrimination with sufficient specificity to justify" majority-Black districts as a defense to potential VRA lawsuits. The conservative majority said the legislature didn't "classify individuals based upon race to an extent greater than reasonably necessary to comply with … the VRA."

The justices also rejected the argument that legislators had violated the state constitution by failing to keep counties whole. Beasley again dissented and argued the court had misinterpreted the U.S. Supreme Court's recent decisions on majority-Black districts in other Southern states.

The state supreme court's decision wouldn't be the last word. Earls argued in federal court, many times, that the districts violated the VRA and the 14th Amendment to the U.S. Constitution by discriminating against Black voters. Farr defended the legislature and repeatedly tried to get federal judges to defer to the state court's rulings. In one brief, he argued that the federal case "never should have been allowed to proceed in the first place."

CHAPTER 5

CARVING UP
URBAN AREAS

In 2011, Earls represented the North Carolina NAACP and voters who sued the Republican legislature in federal court. She challenged the new districts for congressional and legislative elections under the VRA and the 14th Amendment to the U.S. Constitution. North Carolina's Black voters had been unnecessarily packed into districts where they were a majority, reducing their influence in other districts.

Before the 2011 redistricting, none of the 50 districts in the state senate had a majority of Black voters. But the new districts included nine. Professor Irving Joyner of N.C. Central University law school, who advised the North Carolina NAACP, said the VRA "does not compel the drawing of majority-minority districts... It only says that you can't draw lines that would dilute the Black vote."

Rucho and Lewis had outsourced the drawing of the districts to Thomas Hofeller, a redistricting guru who helped Republicans across the U.S. gerrymander elections. The two legislators released

Hofeller's maps, and Republicans tweaked them before passing them on party lines.

Two decades after the U.S. Supreme Court had castigated legislators for drawing a 12th congressional district that resembled "political apartheid," Republicans created a similar, serpentine district to encompass Black voters in several cities. It became slimmer as it crossed the middle of the state diagonally. The district returned to the status of "majority-minority," even though it had—for the past decade—elected a Black candidate without a Black majority.

The 1st district, which includes the majority-Black counties in the Northeastern corner of the state, also became a majority-Black district again. The new district looked like a crustacean, washed up from the Atlantic, with jagged appendages reaching through dozens of rural counties. One of its claws reached South to encompass voters in the city of Durham and the Raleigh suburbs.

These majority-Black districts were good for Republicans, and Farr attributed the unusual shape of the 1st district to partisan, rather than racial, gerrymandering. Legislators claimed they were gerrymandering Democrats, not Black voters.

Farr accused Earls' clients of seeking to "maximize Democratic partisan advantage." For the serpentine 12th district, Farr again argued that the VRA required legislators to pack Black voters into districts where they were a majority.

Republicans maintained their stance, without providing evidence that a Black majority was necessary. Farr told the judges, "We do not think it's a racial gerrymander to draw a 50 percent district." Ken Raymond, a Black Republican, wrote an op-ed calling on Barber and other civil rights leaders to support the GOP's map because "it's clearly in favor of the Black community."

Earls pleaded with federal courts to overturn the North Carolina Supreme Court's decision. She again argued that any additional "packing" of African-American voters, beyond what was necessary, was unconstitutional discrimination.

In court and in public, Republicans pointed out that their districts had been "precleared" by the U.S. Department of Justice under Section 5 of the VRA, which required states with a history of voting discrimination to have changes to elections cleared by the Department or a federal court. Barber argued, however, that the Department had only assessed whether the plan would result in fewer districts that allowed Black voters to elect their preferred candidates. Barber said the Department hadn't studied how the new districts impacted Black voting power in other districts.

Reflecting on the case, Earls said she was optimistic about her clients' chances after Hofeller's testimony. Hofeller talked with ease about drawing districts for various racial groups, with "no appreciation for principles of inclusion or democracy," Earls said, and one of the judges seemed shocked at his "obviously anti-democratic" principles.

Hofeller also made it clear that lawmakers had instructed him to draw a majority-Black 1st congressional district, undermining their claim that the district was a partisan gerrymander. He described how he had made the sprawling 1st district even less compact as he sought a majority-Black population. Testimony from other experts made it clear that Black voters, not Democrats, were the targets of gerrymandering.

Civil rights advocates were appalled that Republicans used the VRA to justify racial gerrymandering. "Republicans in the South have cynically used the Voting Rights Act to justify redistricting for their political advantage," Earls argued. "Political life in North Carolina has evolved since those days when African Americans needed to be more than 50 percent of a district's population in order to have a chance of electing a candidate of their choice."

To get fairer districts, Earls and her cocounsel would ultimately have to convince the conservative majority on the U.S.

Supreme Court. The litigation over North Carolina's 2011 maps took years, and Republicans maintained their supermajority in the state legislature. They exercised every opportunity to delay the litigation. And in the meantime, they had a plan to stay in power by disenfranchising Black voters.

CHAPTER 6

KEEPING BLACK PEOPLE FROM CASTING THEIR BALLOTS

On June 25, 2013, the U.S. Supreme Court convened for the final day of its term, and the justices' decision that day would allow the North Carolina legislature to engage in a shocking attack on voting rights—a modern-day Jim Crow law.

As the sun rose outside the Court, well-dressed spectators waited in line in swamp-like weather, nearly 80 degrees and as humid as it gets. Most of them anticipated that the Court was going to strike down Section 5 of the Voting Rights Act (VRA), which required states with a history of voting discrimination to have new election laws approved by the federal government.

After surrendering their phones and laptops, the spectators filed into the august courtroom and filled the rows of chairs. Some whispered to their neighbors, and others scanned summaries of the case or briefs filed by the parties.

The marshall announced that Court was in session, and the robed justices took their seats. Chief Justice John Roberts announced that the first decision was the VRA case, and he had written the ruling. The voting rights advocates in the room knew that was bad. Roberts had argued against a bill expanding the scope of the VRA as a young lawyer in the Reagan administration. He had said that violations of the VRA "provide a basis for the most intrusive interference imaginable by federal courts into state and local process."

Roberts rose from his chair in the middle of the nine justices and read a summary of the Court's decision in *Shelby County v. Holder*. He said that Congress couldn't apply Section 5 to states that discriminated in 1965, when the law was passed, because "things have changed." Roberts said, "Today the Nation is no longer divided along those lines, yet the Voting Rights Act continues to treat it as if it were."

Justice Ruth Bader Ginsburg was wearing her "dissent collar," a jabot that told the crowd to expect a dissenting opinion from the Notorious RBG. When Roberts finished, Ginsburg rose from her chair.

She began, "In the Court's view, the very success of Section 5 of the Voting Rights Act demands its dormancy. Congress was of another mind. Recognizing that large progress has been made, Congress determined, based on a voluminous record, that the scourge of discrimination was not yet extirpated." Ginsburg argued the majority's decision to strike down Section 5 is like "throwing out your umbrella in a rainstorm, because you are not getting wet."

Earls had filed a brief with the court, arguing that states covered by Section 5, which were mostly in the South, still engaged in more voting discrimination than other states. Ginsburg agreed and noted that there were more state laws blocked under Section 5 between 1982 and 2004 than there were between 1965 and the 1982 reauthorization of the VRA.

The Court had also heard from U.S. Rep. John Lewis, a civil rights activist who was beaten by Alabama police at a voting rights march, days before the VRA was introduced in Congress. He noted the "high price many paid for the enactment of the Voting Rights Act and the still higher cost we might yet bear if we prematurely discard one of the most vital tools of our democracy."

The decision would empower legislators who were already intent on suppressing the vote. In *Give Us the Ballot*, Ari Berman noted that after the GOP's 2010 victories in state legislatures, "half the states in the country, nearly all of them under Republican control—from Texas to Wisconsin to Pennsylvania—passed laws making it harder to vote."

Without Section 5, the problem would get worse. And Rev. Barber warned, "North Carolina is the poster child."

Responding to the Court's decision in Raleigh, state Senator Tom Apodaca said Republicans had anticipated the demise of Section 5. A GOP leader, Apodaca had been spearheading the push for a new voter ID bill. The state House had passed a bill that allowed voters to use a wide range of IDs, including student IDs. But after *Shelby County*, Republicans began to think bigger.

Apodaca ominously said that since the Section 5 "headache" was out of the way, "now we can go with the full bill." Democratic legislators received a copy of the full legislation on the night of July 22, 2013. Republicans scheduled a vote the next day.

The bill went far beyond other states' voter ID laws. The wide-ranging legislation made it harder to vote in several ways, including a voter ID mandate and cuts to early voting.

Republicans had requested data from the state DMV and elections board. An aide for then-House Speaker Thom Tillis, who is now a U.S. Senator, asked for "a breakdown, by race, of those registered voters in your database that do not have a driver's license number." According to a *Washington Post* report on the emails, one Republican lawmaker asked for data on how many people voted outside their precinct. A legislative staffer asked for "a break-down of the 2008 voter turnout, by race (white and Black) and type of vote (early and Election Day)."

Republican legislators then used this information to craft a law that would make it harder for Black people to vote. They asked for data about the types of IDs possessed by Black voters, so they could exclude them from the list of acceptable IDs. Farr helped them sort through this data and write the law, according to the *New York Times Magazine.*

The bill also cut early voting, including one of the two Sundays, when Black churches ran "souls to the polls" operations. It allowed more voters to be "challenged" on whether they were qualified or purged from the registration rolls for inactivity. The bill also eliminated Election Day registration, pre-registration for 16- and 17-year olds, and out-of-precinct voting.

Republicans planned to approve the bill within a week of its unveiling. And Black legislators were appalled. Democratic Rep. Mickey Michaux, Jr., who had served in the legislature for decades, warned that history was "repeating itself." Through tears, Michaux implored Republicans to stop attacking the voting rights that "many of us ... gave our lives for." He pleaded with them to confine the bill to "hell for the rest of eternity."

Voting rights advocates were appalled at the blatant attack on democracy. Earls warned, "We will see long lines, many citizens turned away and not allowed to vote, more provisional ballots cast but many fewer counting, vigilante observers at the polling place and all disproportionately impacting Black voters." Tens of thousands of poor voters could be impacted. "The depth and breadth of the anti-democratic policy is pretty stunning," Earls said.

Rev. Barber and his allies launched a series of weekly protests, drawing thousands of people to the capitol. Activists were arrested during a sit-in protest at Tillis' office.

The bill erased North Carolina's gains in making voting and

registration easier, undoing reforms that Barber and others had pushed the legislature to pass. The 2013 bill was compared to Jim Crow laws, designed to impact Black voters without explicitly mentioning them.

The bill was passed three days after it was introduced, and Gov. McCrory signed it into law. McCrory defended the bill as a safeguard to prevent fraud and downplayed the burden on Black, poor, or young voters. But Carter Wrenn, a longtime GOP operative who worked closely with Farr's former law partner, acknowledged that the law discriminated against Black voters. "Look, if African Americans voted overwhelmingly Republican, they would have kept early voting right where it was," he said.

The North Carolina legislature became the face of modern-day voter suppression.

The state NAACP immediately filed lawsuits in state and federal court challenging the law. Barber said the bill "tramples on the blood of our martyrs" and "desecrates the graves of freedom fighters." Professor Joyner warned that older African Americans in rural North Carolina would be unable to get the required ID: "In a rural state like North Carolina, particularly a state that was steeped in Jim Crow laws, many of the African-Americans affected were born in the '40s, '50s and '60s and don't have a birth certificate."

The state League of Women Voters also filed suit, along with voters who lacked the required ID, and they were represented by Earls' organization, SCSJ. The plaintiffs had the backing of the Department of Justice, which argued the law was intentionally discriminatory.

The legislature was again defended by Farr, who had helped write the bill. He argued that comparing the law to those of the Jim Crow era was "ludicrous."

In the fall of 2013, the trial was held in a federal courthouse in Winston-Salem. Plaintiff Rosanell Eaton, who was nearly 90 years old, testified about passing a literacy test the first time she registered to vote in eastern North Carolina. Eaton said she became an advocate "because my foreparents ... didn't have the opportunity of registering and voting." She went on to register thousands of voters in her community. Eaton had been arrested during a recent protest, getting into "good trouble," as John Lewis called it.

Carolyn Coleman, a 72-year-old Black woman, spoke about her history of advocating for voting rights as former head of the state NAACP. "Everything that I worked for for the last fifty years was being lost," she testified. An expert witness said that Black voters were twice as likely to take advantage of early voting, Election Day registration, and out-of-precinct voting.

The judge, a Republican appointee, upheld the law, and the plaintiffs appealed to the 4th U.S. Circuit Court of Appeals. On October 1, weeks before Election Day 2014, the 4th Circuit blocked the provisions eliminating Election Day registration and out-of-precinct voting.

On October 10, the U.S. Supreme Court overruled the 4th Circuit. The law would be in effect for the midterms. Justice Ginsburg dissented and said these measures would never have gone into effect if Section 5 hadn't been struck down in *Shelby County*.

Voting rights activists were worried about the impact on the election. The state NAACP had organized the "Moral Freedom Summer 2014" on the fiftieth anniversary of Freedom Summer, when John Lewis and other activists had gone to Mississippi to register voters. During one rally, Barber had asked "How many of you are going to leave here and remember the blood of the martyrs?" Hundreds raised their hands. They registered 5,000 new voters that summer, according to Berman.

Despite their efforts, Democracy North Carolina estimated that tens of thousands of voters were disenfranchised in 2014. The group found that 2,344 voters had their ballots rejected because of the elimination of Election Day registration or out-of-precinct voting. Almost 40 percent of the rejected ballots were cast by Black voters, who accounted for less than a quarter of all voters. In that year's election, Tillis won the race for a U.S. Senate seat by around 48,000 votes.

In 2016, the 4th Circuit heard arguments in the case, which had been assigned to a three-judge panel that included Judge James Wynn, a Black jurist from Eastern North Carolina who was nominated by President Barack Obama after his earlier nomination had been blocked by Sen. Jesse Helms. At a courthouse in Richmond, Virginia, NAACP attorney Penda Hair laid out the implications of the law for certain groups of voters. She argued that lawmakers had singled out Black voters.

Representing the League of Women Voters, SCSJ lawyer Allison Riggs argued the law was unprecedented in the modern era. Riggs, who was mentored by Earls, called the 2013 bill "the first major constriction of access to the polls in North Carolina" since the VRA was passed. She said that after *Shelby County*, "North Carolina picked up where history left off in 1965."

Farr rose to defend the law, which he denied had a disproportionate impact on Black voters. "It was not a nefarious thing," he said. Farr compared the provisions to recent laws in other states, which had been upheld. He suggested that a finding of intentional racial discrimination would break new ground, when it comes to election law changes.

Wynn, a former military judge with an authoritative voice, grilled Farr with a series of questions. He asked Farr about the timing of the expansive bill, so soon after the U.S. Supreme Court struck down Section 5 of the VRA. Farr dismissed Apodaca's statement as "the statement of one senator" that didn't imply discrimination by the entire legislature.

They got into the weeds about the requirements of the VRA. Farr had a knack for making alleged voter suppression sound boring. "I apologize if I'm not clarifying this, as well as ... I might," he said at one point.

Wynn asked Farr whether legislators had data on the racial demographics of voters. When Farr replied affirmatively, the judge asked him why they had that data. Farr responded, "Let me ask you a question, your honor."

Wynn laughed and cut him off. "No, you don't ask me questions," he said. The judge repeated himself.

Farr claimed that it was "prudent" for legislators to ask for the demographic data, so they could avoid any charges of racial discrimination. "If you're concerned about complying with ... laws that prohibit discrimination against minorities, it's prudent to find out to some degree what the racial demographics are," he said.

But Wynn noted that this data showed that the practices limited or eliminated by the bill were the ones used more often by Black voters.

Farr acknowledged that legislators had a report that showed the state Board of Elections had matched DMV records with fewer Black voters than white voters, but he said this didn't prove that those voters lacked acceptable IDs. He claimed the numbers were "inflated." Farr blamed the legislature's cut to early voting on "gamesmanship" by local election officials, suggesting they had manipulated the location of early voting sites.

Farr couldn't tell Wynn why legislators had excluded "public assistance" IDs from the list of acceptable IDs. "Why did they take it out?" Wynn asked. Farr claimed he didn't know.

Talking to a reporter after the arguments, Farr maintained that the law hadn't kept Black voters from casting their ballots. He told a reporter that "African-American turnout increased at a higher rate than white" turnout in the 2014 primary, the first election in which the law was in effect. The trial court had also emphasized turnout when it upheld the law.

The voter ID requirement first went into effect during the

March 2016 primary, and Democracy North Carolina again found that thousands of voters were impacted by the law.

In *Give Us the Ballot*, Berman says other states' voter ID laws went into effect in the 2014 election, and turnout plummeted "to the lowest level since 1942." The U.S. Supreme Court refused to intervene to block most of the laws. The voters who did turn out were older, less diverse, and more conservative than the last two elections. And Berman noted that "the GOP tightened its grip on state governments."

CHAPTER 7

TEN REPUBLICANS AND THREE DEMOCRATS

On February 5, 2016, a federal court ruled that the North Carolina legislature had discriminated against Black voters in drawing the state's congressional election districts. It was a victory for Earls, her cocounsel, and Black voters. But in the end, it wouldn't help break the GOP's stranglehold over election districts.

The decision was written by Judge Roger Gregory, a Black judge whose appointment by President Bill Clinton to the 4th U.S. Circuit Court of Appeals had been delayed until the president's final weeks in office, due to the opposition of Sen. Helms. Gregory's opinion for a three-judge panel discussed the history of the serpentine-shaped 12th district.

The court noted that Rep. Watt, the candidate supported by Black voters, had been re-elected comfortably several times without a majority-Black district. Gregory described the "strong evidence that race was the only nonnegotiable criterion" in Hofeller's mapmaking, and he cited "overwhelming evidence" of a "racial quota" in the 1st and 12th districts. Judge William Osteen, a Republican appointee, dissented and argued that race wasn't the "predominant" motive in drawing the 12th district.

Rev. Barber called the decision a victory "against 21st-century racism and discrimination." But the leaders of the Republican caucus, Sen. Bob Rucho and Rep. David Lewis, issued a statement suggesting that the ruling would lead to chaos in the upcoming primary election. They claimed the ruling "could do far more to disenfranchise North Carolina voters than anything alleged in this case."

The U.S. Supreme Court declined to overturn the decision. So on the afternoon of Friday, February 12, Republicans announced that they would redraw election districts. They would hear public comments on Monday.

That weekend, a winter storm covered most of North Carolina's roads in ice. But lawmakers in Raleigh plowed ahead. They allowed citizens to offer public comments by calling in from half a dozen locations across the state. The call-in location in Greensboro was closed, due to the icy roads.

Legislators got an earful from Gary Grant, whose family had settled in majority-Black Halifax County through a New Deal-era program that helped Black families purchase farms in the town of Tillery. Grant had complained to Republican legislators when the 1st congressional district was drawn in 2011, and he accused them of once again "cramming Black people" into one district.

Grant rejected legislators' justifications and called on them to make the districts fair. "It's a mess. You made it. Clean it up," he demanded. Other citizens were just as angry.

The next day, the joint house/senate redistricting committee met at the capitol. The mostly male group of legislators sat in rows of tables, facing the front podium. Rucho and Lewis kicked things off by discussing the criteria that would be used to draw the new districts. Legislators approved noncontroversial criteria, such as equal population.

Sen. Blue, the minority leader, asked Lewis about the use of demographic data. "Race is not to be a factor in drawing the districts," Lewis responded. Blue asked him to clarify if he was actually saying that, after the court's finding of racial gerrymandering, legislators planned to completely ignore the impact of the districts on Black voters.

"I don't think it's wise to spit in the eyes of three federal judges who control the fate of where we're going to go with redistricting," Blue said. "I think it's an insult to their intelligence to take this approach."

Republicans approved the no-racial-data criterion. Then Lewis had legislative staff hand out copies of a document that explained a criterion titled "partisan advantage." The document said: "The partisan makeup of the congressional delegation under the enacted plan is 10 Republicans and 3 Democrats."

Democrats pointed out that Lewis' proposed districts would perpetuate the same partisan advantage that Republicans had achieved through racial gerrymandering. Sen. Floyd McKissick noted that the state's voters were nearly evenly split between Republicans and Democrats. He asked, "I'm trying to understand why you feel this would be fair?"

Lewis responded, "Thank you for your question, senator. I propose that we draw the maps to give a partisan advantage to 10 Republicans and 3 Democrats, because I do not think it's possible to draw a map that elects 11 Republicans." The Republicans laughed.

(Years later, Hofeller's hard drive revealed that a more extreme gerrymander was possible. In addition to drawing a map with 11 Republican seats, Hofeller had also drawn districts that likely would have elected an all-white slate to Congress.)

Lewis emphasized that lawmakers were drawing the districts

"to gain partisan advantage." He then looked up from his notes, punctuating each word with his hand. "I want that criteria to be clearly stated and understood," he said.

Lewis deflected objections from Democrats, and his criteria passed along party lines. The next day at 4:00 pm, the committee reconvened. Republicans planned to hold a final vote that night. Sen. Rucho joked about whether they would adjourn in time to watch the Duke-Carolina men's basketball game, which pit bitter rivals against one another.

But Republicans weren't ready to call a vote yet. The copies of the new districts hadn't arrived from the printer. After a brief recess, staffers handed out the maps.

Sen. Blue suggested the new districts were still racially gerrymandered. He said Republicans had "again managed to stuff about half of the Black population in the state" into three districts. By focusing on Democrats but ignoring the impact on Black voters, Blue argued that Republicans were gerrymandering many of the same voters as they had in 2011.

Blue also warned that designing the new districts to skew so far towards Republican candidates was a "direct assault on democracy." He said voters would be furious over the blatant partisan power grab.

During the debates, Sen. Apodaca cracked a joke about how long Rep. Mickey Michaux had served. When Michaux didn't laugh, Apodaca said, "Smile, Mickey."

The districts were approved the next day. The new partisan gerrymander would prove to be ironclad. The 10-3 imbalance would hold through the rest of the decade, even when Democratic candidates got more total votes. Democratic candidates in North Carolina would win only three seats in Congress, whether they received 44 percent of the vote or 51 percent.

Soon after they created the 10-3 districts, legislators found themselves back in Raleigh to redraw more districts. In August

2016, Judge Wynn wrote a decision striking down dozens of state legislative election districts for discriminating against Black voters. In addition to congressional seats, the legislature had racially gerrymandered its own districts. Wynn noted the absence of any evidence that legislators had targeted Democrats, and he outlined the "copious" evidence that they had targeted Black voters.

The court said that no one besides Lewis, Rucho, and Hofeller "had any substantive role in designing the districts." Wynn's ruling quoted the legislators' interpretation of the VRA and said, "This is not a proper interpretation of the law."

Legislators hadn't even asked if majority-Black districts were necessary to avoid diluting Black voters' political power. The court ruled the districts unconstitutional but lamented that there wasn't enough time to fix them before the 2016 election. The judges did, however, order a special election the following year.

In the spring of 2017, the U.S. Supreme Court upheld the decisions to strike down both the legislative and congressional districts. In an unsigned decision with no dissents, the justices also overturned the lower court's order requiring special legislative elections that year.

Justice Elena Kagan, an Obama appointee, wrote the decision in May on the congressional districts. The Court said legislators had chosen to grow the 12th district by taking "people from heavily Black areas of Durham, requiring a finger-like extension of the district's western line." The decision, which was joined by Justice Clarence Thomas, rejected the legislature's VRA justification. Commentator Elie Mystal noted that legislators hadn't engaged in "any kind of inquiry into the political make-up of those districts: they just kind of noticed that there were a lot of Black people in those districts and essentially tried to ghettoize them."

In June 2017, Republicans redrew their legislative election districts to undo their racial gerrymander. And this time, lawmakers didn't announce the election results that their new districts would guarantee. The criteria didn't include "partisan advantage" but did include "political considerations."

As lawmakers redistricted, Earls wrote a letter to Farr and warned that some of the new districts were still unconstitutional. But lawmakers didn't alter them.

Though the court had only struck down 28 districts, the legislature redrew 116 districts. And Earls argued that some of the new districts in cities like Charlotte and Greensboro still discriminated against Black voters. Republicans claimed the majority-Black districts were "naturally occurring." But Earls had only objected to the districts that were misshapen or skewed in a clear gerrymander.

The court ended up redrawing four districts with the help of an expert, who did not unnecessarily pack Black voters into a handful of districts. After years of litigation, the state's congressional and legislative districts had been redrawn to be fairer to Black voters.

In Judge Wynn's decision conceding that a special election was impossible, he emphasized the "widespread, serious, and long-standing" effects of the racial gerrymander. Beyond the immediate harm to "voters who were unjustifiably placed within and without districts based on the color of their skin, plaintiffs—along with millions of North Carolinians of all races—have lived and continue to live under laws adopted by a state legislature elected from unconstitutionally drawn districts."

The court declined to rule that the gerrymandered legislature lacked authority to govern, with Judge Wynn noting that its authority to legislate was an "unsettled question of state law" that should be decided by state courts.

Despite Black voters' victory in court, the party that most of them supported still had no real chance of governing the state legislature. The districts were still slanted toward the GOP. That's why Earls would file a new lawsuit challenging the new districts on the basis of partisan, not racial, gerrymandering.

The U.S. Supreme Court had previously ruled that partisan

gerrymandering claims were beyond the reach of federal courts. But there was a growing recognition around the country of the unfairness inherent in the post-2010 congressional districts. When Earls' lawsuit arrived at the nation's highest Court, it would be combined with another suit challenging gerrymandering by a Democratic state legislature.

Voters in many states had created independent, bipartisan commissions to handle redistricting. That wasn't an option in North Carolina, where only the legislature can introduce constitutional amendments. And voters were becoming increasingly outraged at the unaccountable, all-white GOP majority that ruled the state.

CHAPTER 8

FORWARD TOGETHER

The legislature's ruthless voter suppression ignited a fire of protest that would burn outside the capitol for years. Rev. Barber, who was president of the North Carolina NAACP, had spent years working with allies to build an intersectional movement. And in 2013, Barber's coalition organized the "Moral Monday" rallies to let the gerrymandered legislature know that it could still be held accountable.

On a chilly February morning in 2013, thousands of North Carolinians gathered on Jones Street, outside the capitol in Raleigh. They carried signs demanding voting rights and access to healthcare. Local NAACP chapters carried yellow and blue banners. A young Black man held a sign that read, "Poverty is the worst type of violence," next to a young white woman with a sign quoting Jesus' call to help "the least of these."

The people crowded onto the sidewalk and into the street. They faced a stage in front of the capitol, where the reverend was getting ready to preach. Barber started by calling on the crowd to look around and notice the diversity in their ranks.

Barber then listed a series of policy demands that would help poor people, an agenda based on "nonpartisan human values." He demanded living wages, a green economy, affordable housing, fair policies for immigrants, and more. "We have to have educational equality, ensure that every child has a well-funded, constitutional, diverse public education," Barber inveighed. He called on the crowd to demand voting rights and "fairness in the criminal justice system."

Barber's voice grew louder as the list grew longer. He talked most about poverty. "Our purpose is to mourn the grim reality of so many North Carolinians in poverty." Barber rattled off statistics that laid bare the growing income inequality, as well as the racial wealth gap and widespread child poverty that existed in the state.

"These are not Black or white children. They're *our* children!" he exclaimed.

The reverend talked about what he saw when touring the state to survey poverty. "We saw people living in the woods, living in storm drains, trying to make it," he said. "We cannot ignore this issue. These are our brothers and sisters." Barber called on the crowd to repeat the last line. He criticized recent legislation that inflicted "violence on the poor."

In his thundering "preaching voice," Barber called out the GOP legislature for refusing to provide healthcare to citizens in need. He described their justifications for inaction as a "strange tongue" that he couldn't understand. "It does not sound like freedom, does not sound like justice, does not sound like righteousness!" He described the legislature's economic agenda as "morally unconscionable," a "Robin Hood in reverse."

The reverend said they wouldn't be deterred by the fact that Republicans held a gerrymandered supermajority in the legislature. "Slavery had a supermajority. But Harriet Tubman didn't care nothin' about that. And freedom came."

"We are called to bear witness at this moment in history. We have faith that there's a better way for North Carolina, and a better way for America, and a better way for our world," he said.

If voters couldn't be heard through the ballot box, Barber made sure they would be heard in the streets outside the capitol and, when necessary, in the galleries above the house and senate chambers.

Drawing on his faith, Barber would lead thousands of marchers and supporters. He led rallies across North Carolina and preached to the masses about taking care of their fellow man and the immorality of policies that harmed marginalized communities. He would conclude by repeating the group's battle cry: "Forward together!" And the crowd's booming response: "NOT ONE STEP BACK!"

Barber said the phrase was born when a protestor began singing, to the tune of the old spiritual *Wade in the Water,* "Forward together, not one step back. God's gonna trouble the waters."

Starting in April 2013, when the voter ID law was introduced, the protests became more frequent. Dissatisfied North Carolinians gathered outside the legislature every Monday when the legislature was in session.

On April 29, Barber and other faith leaders led a group of citizens to confront their legislators. Historian Timothy Tyson wrote about how he joined the group outside the legislature. They stopped in front of the glass double doors to pray and sing. Security guards asked them to step away from the doors, but they would not be moved.

They were arrested, to the sounds of cheers from their compatriots. Between 2013 and 2015, more than 1,000 protesters, including Rev. Barber and his daughter Rebekah, would be arrested for civil disobedience. And the crowds shouted to them, "Thank you! We love you!"

Before going to the capitol that day, Barber and other faith leaders had published an open letter that called the voter ID bill "the most egregious trampling of democracy." The clergy said, "What we do here today is only what any responsible shepherd does to alert God's flock to the presence of predators of democracy."

The letter said the voter ID bill "will stand before the judgment of our courts. But we cannot wait for the wheels of justice to grind while this legislature grinds up the poor and downtrodden. We have to bear witness to the moral wrong that is being committed here."

On a humid July morning in 2013, as a federal court prepared to judge the new voter ID law, activists gathered on the steps of the courthouse on the bustling Main Street in downtown Winston-Salem, across from the county courthouse and jail. Barber addressed the crowd and chastised the U.S. Supreme Court for weakening the VRA in the *Shelby County* decision.

"On June 26, 2013, we had less voting rights than they had on August 6, 1965," he said. The crowd roared. Barber shouted above the crowd: "Like those who answered Dr. King's call 50 years ago, this is our Selma now!"

Barber wrote to Congress and implored them to overturn the *Shelby County* decision. "Clearly, the avalanche of attacks we are seeing leveled at voting rights and the intense attempts at voter suppression in state houses around the country remain a constant reminder of the constitutional and moral necessity for Section 5 of the Voting Rights Act," he said.

The reverend refused to qualify his description of the legislature's racist voter suppression. "People keep asking, 'When they passed this law, were they racist in their heart?' It doesn't matter," Barber said. "You look at the heart of their policies. If I tell you this law is going to affect Black people more than anyone else, and you still go ahead and do it, you yourself are making clear exactly what you are."

Barber described the legislature's voter suppression agenda partly as a reaction to the election of the first Black president in

2008. He called out the legislature for targeting Black voters, just like the segregationists of the 20th century.

After racist violence failed to turn back the civil rights victories of the 1960s and 1970s, "Jim Crow went to law school and got respectable," Barber said. He often referred to "James Crow, Esquire."

The Moral Monday movement spread to cities throughout the state when the legislature was out of session. Citizens who were fed up with their legislature flocked to Barber's movement. The organizers were pleased at the high turnout for the early events. Barber said, "The incredible thing, the fact that amazed me over and over again, was that it kept happening."

The unaccountable, gerrymandered legislature would feel the impact of this movement. "We did not know how long we would have to struggle or how many obstacles we would have to overcome," Barber wrote in *The Third Reconstruction*. "We had held up our vision and sent out a battle cry. Now we had an army."

People attending Barber's events would be moved to tears by his words. They finally felt heard in his thundering call for justice. They marched with him in cities and towns throughout the state, and eventually, throughout America.

Walking with the help of a cane, Barber's large frame moves slowly, a shuffle resulting from a painful condition that caused his spinal vertebrae to fuse. Barber was born on the weekend of the 1963 March on Washington. He described his parents as activists that "baptized me in the river of resistance." In kindergarten, Barber had integrated a public school in rural Roper, North Carolina. His father was a preacher.

The young Barber initially resisted the idea of becoming a preacher, according to his autobiography. But Barber came to terms with the church and "heard a call to … reclaim moral language in the public square." In 2005, he became the leader of the North Carolina NAACP, promising that the organization would "reinsert itself in the matters of our day." Barber and other organizers then spent years building a new intersectional movement on the historical foundation of the early-20th century "Fusion" movement, which brought poor farmers and Black voters together in North Carolina. "We recognized that many of the same political forces that are against, say, gender rights, are often also against education equality, environmental justice, and policies that help the poor," he said.

Barber connected the dots, intersecting the issues facing different communities in North Carolina. "By suppressing our right to vote, they're limiting our ability to fight their attacks on our health care, our labor rights, our taxes, our environment, and the soul of our nation," he wrote in an op-ed. The coalition consisted of more than 140 organizations by 2013.

The movement, as well as Barber's rhetoric, sought to break down the division that pits poor white people against poor people of color—the division that broke the Fusion movement in the early 20th century. "Politicians weren't addressing poor people's concerns, because they knew in a very real sense that they would not have to answer to poor people," he said in his book.

The reverend brought a much-needed moral clarity to North Carolina politics. Barber said, "We saw that every major faith says that love and justice should be at the center of public policy… We had to have a moral challenge because these policies they were passing, in rapid-fire, were constitutionally inconsistent, morally indefensible, and economically insane." Barber helped create a movement that was broader than voting rights.

"Moral Mondays" became citizens' outlet for challenging the legislature, and civil rights veteran Bob Zellner, who advised Barber, said it was "like in the old days." Zellner had been the first white field secretary of the Student Nonviolent Coordinating

Committee, and he was beaten during protests alongside John Lewis. He later moved to the town of Wilson, not far from Barber's home in Goldsboro. Marching with Barber in 2013, Zellner felt like the movement of the 1960s was reborn: "We've been waiting for a renewal of the civil rights movement, and this is it."

The movement was a response to the Republican legislature's far-right agenda. In 2013, lawmakers repealed the Racial Justice Act, which sought to address the longstanding problem of Black people being sentenced to death by all-white juries. A 2014 rally brought out more than 100,000 people, in what was then the largest protest for racial justice since the 1960s. The legislature also passed a bill in 2015 prohibiting the removal of Confederate monuments. In the coming years, protesters would tear many of them down anyway.

Barber's coalition grew larger as other marginalized communities were targeted. The legislature angered many voters when they passed H.B. 2, the notorious 2016 "bathroom bill" that drove new activists to oppose the legislature. The city of Charlotte had passed a civil rights law specifying that transgender people could use the bathroom that corresponds to their gender identity.

In the middle of the night, legislators in Raleigh passed a law that required transgender people to use the bathroom corresponding to the gender they were assigned at birth. The bill went even further and banned all local civil rights laws.

The *New York Times* called out Republicans for peddling false claims about "transgender women as potential rapists. That threat exists only in the imaginations of bigots." Legislators couldn't point to an example that justified their new restrictions on who could use which toilet. "By promoting the ludicrous idea that transgender women are inherently dangerous, the law endangers citizens who are already disproportionately vulnerable to violence and stigmatization," the *Times* noted.

Transgender people were facing the vilest slanders in the halls of the capitol. And in Charlotte, transgender teens were killing themselves by walking onto busy highways. One of them had been crowned homecoming king in high school and was enrolled in college.

Equality NC, a LGBTQ+ rights organization, called for a boycott. Corporations and sporting events refused to do business in the state. The NCAA college basketball tournaments pulled out of the state, home of the "Tobacco Road" rivalry between Duke and the University of North Carolina-Chapel Hill (UNC).

Barber said the law was "not just about bathrooms; it's about whether you can codify hate and discrimination into the laws of the state." The bill not only discriminated against transgender people, it also banned local minimum wage increases and eliminated state civil rights laws, which Farr called a "better policy."

Republican legislation also targeted poor people. UNC law professor Gene Nichol wrote in his book, *Indecent Assembly*, "Poor Tar Heels have been targeted, demonized, shamed, and economically penalized—essentially treated as outcasts to the commonwealth—deserving disdain rather than brotherhood." North Carolina became the first state to repeal an Earned Income Tax Credit, which offered a tax break to low-income families. They raised taxes on the poorest residents and lowered taxes for the wealthy.

Nichol's book also catalogued the legislature's attacks on public education and environmental protections. The legislature cracked down on lawsuits filed by residents of Eastern North Carolina, many of them Black, against factory farms that polluted the air and water.

In 2013, all of the top leaders in the legislature—of both parties—were men, and Republicans attacked women's rights through a late-night amendment to a motorcycle safety bill. The amendment was an example of a targeted regulation of abortion providers (TRAP) law intended to limit access to abortion.

Legislators didn't have to worry about how the voters felt about these bills, because they had gerrymandered their way out of any accountability.

But Barber made sure they would be held to a higher standard. He joined with clergy from other denominations and faiths to condemn immoral laws. "Each of us had a tradition we held dear and a message we shared with our flock on Friday, Saturday, or Sunday. We weren't giving any of that up. But on Monday, we were learning to stand together and proclaim the deepest shared values of our faith tradition. We were learning how those values were embedded in our state constitution."

Barber often quoted the state constitution, "We read where it says that in North Carolina, all political power should only be used for the good of the whole." Citizens also have a right to "instruct" their legislature in North Carolina, and Barber's movement was relentless in its efforts to demand that Republicans stop their immoral power grabs.

The NAACP filed lawsuit after lawsuit to vindicate voters' rights under the state constitution. The reverend understood the importance of the courts in the fight for justice and equality. As Barber's movement spread and he became a national figure, he found himself returning to the capitol to stop the legislature's schemes to take over the courts.

In his book, Barber described the right-wing establishment they faced. At the center of it was Art Pope, the millionaire campaign donor. "Off the record, in secret meetings with power brokers across the state, Pope was plotting a takeover of North Carolina's government," he said. In 2013, Pope played a pivotal role in the legislature's first big change to judicial elections. Barber writes that Republicans "moved to end public financing for judicial elections, which would allow them to buy off judges to influence them to refuse our challenges to their unconstitutional actions."

PART II

BATTLE FOR THE COURTS

CHAPTER 9

UNLEVELING THE PLAYING FIELD

Only two countries in the world, the U.S. and Bolivia, elect judges. Most U.S. states elect their judges, and in 2012, only one state—North Carolina—had an effective public financing system that allowed judicial candidates to avoid raising large campaign contributions from lawyers and corporations. This system would be tested by an influx of GOP campaign cash in the 2012 election, and soon after that, it would be eliminated by the 2013 voter suppression law.

From 2004 to 2012, candidates for the state supreme court or court of appeals could qualify for public campaign funds by raising a certain number of small contributions. Eighty percent of appellate court candidates—Republicans and Democrats—participated. A poll found that more than two-thirds of North Carolina voters supported the program, and less than a quarter opposed it. The system helped foster racial diversity on appellate courts by leveling the playing field for candidates who lacked connections to wealthy, white donors.

The public financing system had been created after the 2000 North Carolina Supreme Court election, in which candidates raised more than $2 million, a record amount. Judge James Wynn, who was then a member of the Court of Appeals, had supported the reform. He compared judges relying on large donors to letting "baseball players contribute money to influence the selection of umpires." The program served as a model for reforms in other states.

Both candidates in the 2012 North Carolina Supreme Court race—conservative Justice Paul Newby and challenger Sam Ervin IV, the son of a U.S. Senator who played a prominent role in the Watergate hearings—had accepted public funds. They both ran ads touting their qualifications and promising to be fair.

Newby was trailing in the polls as the election neared. But on November 2, just days before Election Day, a new group called Justice for All NC began airing an ad attacking Ervin's record and tying him to a convicted former governor. The ad featured an ominous black-and-white picture of the state supreme court, the portraits of former chief justices looming over the bench. The ad then asked, "Can we trust him … to be a fair judge?" Justice for All NC concluded by announcing its sponsorship of the ad, over a color image of a smiling blonde woman holding a baby.

Justice for All NC received more than $1 million that year from the Republican State Leadership Committee (RSLC), which had just helped the GOP take over the legislature and gerrymander elections. The 2012 supreme court race was the first judicial election in which the RSLC had funded ads. The group, as well as Justice for All NC, also gave big to a group that aired an ad supporting Newby.

Money from the RSLC overwhelmed the public financing system. Newby and Ervin each received around $240,000 in public financing. Both candidates would have received additional "matching" public funds, but the U.S. Supreme Court had struck down such systems, construing them as a "penalty" on money spent by independent groups like the RSLC (since money equals speech at the Court). A think tank funded by Art Pope had made a similar argument.

Groups funded by the RSLC and big business poured in more than $2 million—nearly ten times the amount of public financing for each candidate—to help Newby, who won by a few percentage points. Ervin said he believed that the RSLC's ad was the first attack ad in a North Carolina judicial race.

The RSLC was funded that year with donations from large pharmaceutical and fossil fuel companies, among others. A North Carolina-based tobacco company gave the group around $1 million.

After the RSLC's money swamped the election, Republicans sought to defund the public financing program in their June 2013 budget. Pope was hired to be Gov. McCrory's budget director after funding the GOP takeover, and he helped craft a budget bill that cut the program's funding, which had come from attorneys' fees and a voluntary $3 check-off on state income tax returns.

Melissa Kromm was the head of N.C. Voters for Clean Elections, which was created to push for the public financing program in 1999, just as judicial elections around the country were suddenly facing a flood of corporate campaign cash. She lobbied legislators on both sides of the aisle to save the program.

Kromm's Southern drawl was thick and unabashed. She had grown up outside of Raleigh, on the edge of Eastern North Carolina. Her parents were Democrats, and her father had run for a seat in the state legislature. When Kromm was in high school, her mom had informed the family that she was running for a seat on the local school board. "We were at dinner, and my mom just put down the mashed potatoes, and said 'I'm doing it'," Kromm recalled. Her parents' political activism inspired her.

She graduated from N.C. State University in Raleigh in 2006, then went to work as a political consultant. Kromm then got a job working with a law firm that did election law, and this led her to her job leading N.C. Voters for Clean Elections.

Kromm had known that Pope didn't like the public financing program. His network of think tanks had criticized it, and Kromm knew they would have to fight to save the program. "When the sugar daddy of the legislature comes to cut your program, you know it's going to be a big fight," she said in a recent interview.

When Pope presented the governor's proposed budget, he singled out public financing for elimination. "It was such a small thing to just point out in one of these big overviews of the budget," Kromm said.

She was working with GOP Rep. Jonathan Jordan on a compromise to keep funding the program. Kromm said Jordan was about to introduce an amendment to restore funding, when Pope entered the house chamber, ran up the stairs, and summoned Jordan. After their discussion, Jordan pulled the amendment.

Kromm said no one else spoke up to save the program's funding. "I was really scared, because I was the only one willing to say this happened," she said. Kromm conferred with her husband Chris, the publisher of the online magazine *Facing South*, and he wrote a story about the death of public financing. After that, "it became a national news story," she recalled. Chris' story said that the governor's budget director preferred "Pope-funded elections" to public financing.

The governor's budget became law.

A few weeks later, Republicans added a provision to the 2013 voter suppression bill that would kill public financing for good. It was on page 40 of the 49-page legislation. And given the attention on the measures that restricted access to voting, the repeal of public financing didn't generate as much outrage.

After the bill passed, Kromm lobbied legislators to restore the program. And new research supported the case for public financing. A 2014 report by the Center for American Progress (CAP) in Washington, D.C., examined the success rates of law firms that contributed money to the justices' campaigns. For firms that were "repeat players," with five cases or more before the high courts, their average success rates were correlated with how much they had donated to the justices' campaigns.

In 1998, before the program existed, the repeat-player firms that gave more than $400 had a 70 percent success rate, compared to 33 percent for firms that donated less than $400 to the justices. In 2004, the first year that public funds were available, the success rate for repeat players giving more than $400 fell to 61 percent. A 2012 report from the same group showed that, in most of the states with multimillion-dollar judicial elections, the high courts were more likely to rule for corporations and against injured workers and consumers.

In 2014, after the repeal of public financing, North Carolina Supreme Court candidates had to raise large campaign contributions—a record $5 million. The election also saw spending by many of the same independent groups that spent big in 2012. The RSLC funded another ad from Justice for All NC, this time attacking Justice Robin Hudson for ruling in favor of "child molesters." These "soft on crime" attack ads had been shown to create pressure on judges to rule against criminal defendants. The RSLC's ad failed to unseat Hudson.

Given the flood of campaign cash since the end of public financing, activists called on the legislature to create a new small-donor matching system, which multiplies small donations with public funds, as long as candidates don't take larger donations. Small-donor matching can help ensure that publicly financed candidates stay competitive when facing millions of dollars in independent spending.

The high court election again saw millions of dollars in 2016, when the state Chamber of Commerce spent big to support the conservative incumbent. The group's spokesperson suggested the incumbent would rule to limit legal liability for corporations.

Former Justice Bob Orr said the increased spending in high court races by outside groups "all revolves around redistricting." The RSLC had helped elect a GOP majority and then helped that majority gerrymander elections to preserve its power, regardless of what the voters wanted. The RSLC then spent big to maintain a conservative majority on the North Carolina Supreme Court, so that it wouldn't undo their skewed election districts.

CHAPTER 10

WHEN THE MAP-DRAWERS FUND JUDICIAL CAMPAIGNS

Norto Carolina was the first state in which the RSLC spent money in a judicial race. And the group's money created a glaring conflict of interest when the state supreme court was deciding whether the legislature had discriminated against Black voters when drawing election districts. (*See Chapter 4.*)

The RSLC's shift to spending in judicial elections was spearheaded by the group's president, Chris Jankowski. And when the RSLC established a political action committee (PAC) in North Carolina, Jankowski signed the paperwork.

Jankowski had begun his career lobbying for insurance companies in the 1990s, and in that role, he realized the importance of state courts. The "tort reform" movement was in full swing, pushing for limits on lawsuits filed by injured workers and consumers. The groups were funded by insurers, pharmaceutical companies, and Big Tobacco—corporations that didn't like paying jury verdicts when their products harmed people. They set up fake grassroots organizations and funded propaganda about "frivolous lawsuits," even though the most common tort reform laws only apply in cases with the most severe injuries.

Jankowski argued that lawsuits against corporations were "extortion," and the insurance industry had realized that "we've got to change these courts." In an interview with Daley in *Ratf*cked*, Jankowski said he pitched that idea to insurance company CEOs and the U.S. Chamber of Commerce, who all signed on. He worked with GOP consultant Karl Rove, who had run campaigns in the 1990s that flipped the Texas and Alabama Supreme Courts from all-Democrat to all-Republican.

In the coming years, the Chamber and its state affiliates would dominate high court elections around the country. The Chamber's Institute for Legal Reform would become one of the RSLC's biggest donors as it lobbied for bills restricting lawsuits by injured workers and consumers.

The RSLC poured $1.2 million into the 2012 race for a seat on the North Carolina Supreme Court, which would soon hear a lawsuit challenging the gerrymandered election districts that the RSLC had helped to draw.

In the wake of the *Shelby County* decision, state supreme courts became more important to protecting the right to vote. But in many of the states where legislators restricted the right to vote, the Chamber and the RSLC had spent millions of dollars to make sure conservative judges control high courts.

When the gerrymandering case reached the North Carolina Supreme Court, the NAACP asked Newby to recuse himself, due to the RSLC's spending on his behalf and its role in drawing the districts. Kromm and others also called on Newby to sit out the case.

Earls and her co-counsel argued that "unless Justice Newby recuses himself, he will rule on the validity of redistricting plans that were drawn, endorsed, and embraced by the principal funder of a committee supporting his campaign for re-election." Their brief warned that the conflict of interest had "created a widespread and persisting perception that Newby is likely to be predisposed to uphold" the districts. In 2009, the U.S. Supreme Court had required a high court justice to sit out a case involving a campaign donor that played a critical role in getting him elected.

In response, Farr and his team argued that the recusal request "seeks to insert politics where it does not belong, in the judicial process." He accused the plaintiffs and their lawyers of "unnecessarily question[ing] the integrity of this court" and said they had unfairly suggested the case would "be decided based upon political allegiances, rather than the law and facts." Farr said Republican legislators had "complete confidence" that Newby would decide the case fairly.

In a one-sentence order on December 17, 2012, the state supreme court denied the motion for recusal. It was signed by conservative Justice Barbara Jackson. The conflict of interest issue came up again, after the U.S. Supreme Court ordered the justices in Raleigh to reconsider their ruling. The court again denied the NAACP's request.

After Newby was reelected with the RSLC's help in 2012, he lobbied legislators to change the process for handling ethics complaints against judges. His effort was joined by conservative Justice Mark Martin, according to NC Policy Watch. The bill put the high court justices in charge of policing their own compliance with ethical rules, instead of having a panel of appellate judges do it.

The Democratic chief justice opposed the change, but a Republican legislator said a majority of the court supported it. Democratic Rep. Rick Glazier called it "a plot to cover up potential claims against sitting justices."

Glazier also spoke out against two things in the 2014 state

budget that made big, non-fiscal changes to Superior Courts, which hear felony criminal trials and civil lawsuits over more than $10,000. One provision eliminated four judgeships, three of which had been filled by a Democratic governor, and required any future appointees to be confirmed by the legislature.

A lawyer from the military community of Fayetteville, Glazier said the confirmation requirement had "just appeared overnight," and he called it a "politicized attack" on the independence of the courts. He argued it was intended to curtail the power of a possible Democratic successor to Gov. McCrory.

Glazier argued the second change to Superior Courts was unconstitutional. This provision would have moved lawsuits challenging state laws from a court in Raleigh to a three-judge panel, appointed by the Chief Justice. At the time, the Democrat chief justice was leaving the court, and the leading candidate to replace her was Justice Martin, a conservative.

During budget debates, Glazier rose from his chair and said the new three-judge panel system was designed to get a court that favored Republicans. "Nobody denied it when I made the accusation," he said.

The changes to Superior Courts mostly flew under the radar. But an article by Jordan Green in the *Triad City Beat* warned that the two budget provisions would "give the Republican-controlled legislature greater influence over the state judiciary and insulate the majority from legal challenges."

Legislators even considered adding two seats to the state supreme court. With the governor filling the seats, the conservative majority would be secure for years. The two seats were in an amendment to an unrelated bill, but they failed to gain enough support in the state house.

Glazier's prediction about a future Democratic governor would prove true, and when that happened, the legislature tried to take the power to fill vacant judicial seats from the executive branch.

The repeal of public financing and the changes to Superior Courts were a glimpse of what was to come for the judicial branch. In the coming years, the legislature would do whatever it took to take control of the courts.

Legislators had read a 2013 memo from consultant John Davis, who had advised them that high courts races were "critical for long-term Republican dominance." Davis titled his memo, "How the North Carolina Republican Party can maintain political power for 114 years," and he called on lawmakers to enact "radical reforms" to the courts and judicial raes.

Most of the power grabs targeted Black judges or judicial candidates, as well as Black voters. And in 2015, all of the top Republican leaders—and two-thirds of the legislature overall— were white men.

In 2016, Republican legislators were facing the prospect that voters that fall would elect a progressive majority to the North Carolina Supreme Court. Judge Mike Morgan, a Black judge in Raleigh, was challenging a conservative incumbent.

Republicans couldn't gerrymander the high court election, which was statewide, so instead they passed a law designed to keep a conservative majority on the court, no matter what the voters decided.

CHAPTER 11

CANCELING THE HIGH COURT ELECTION

With control of the North Carolina Supreme Court up for grabs, lawmakers tried to effectively cancel the 2016 high court election before it happened. In April 2015, as the courts were weighing challenges to their election districts, Republican legislators introduced a law that would have radically changed high court elections.

A conservative justice was on the ballot, two years after Democratic victories in 2014. But the bill would have moved from a system of contested high court elections to one in which voters wouldn't have the chance to elect a progressive majority. They would only decide whether to keep an incumbent in office through a "retention election."

Legislators' intentions were clear. The court would have kept its conservative majority, even if the people had voted out the Republican incumbent. A replacement justice would have been chosen by Gov. McCrory, even if he was voted out in the same election. McCrory's appointee would have served for two years before appearing on the ballot.

The same legislators who eliminated public financing claimed this new system would keep money out of judicial elections. One GOP legislator claimed that voters were tired of "seeing millions of dollars spent electing a member of the Supreme Court or the Court of Appeals."

Critics said the law was clearly an attempt to keep voters from electing Judge Morgan over the incumbent conservative. Kromm charged the legislature with rigging the supreme court election "under the guise that they are trying to get rid of big money in judicial elections." She called it a "partisan, political power grab." Commentator Chris Fitzsimon said there's nothing "inherently partisan" about retention elections. But "it's hard to make a rational argument that they should start immediately with less than a year's notice and with the ideological control of the court at stake."

Voters would have had no real choice in the 2016 race. But a lawyer who said she was interested in running filed a lawsuit in state court. And a panel of three judges ruled that the law violated the N.C. Constitution, which gives voters the right to choose their judges.

The short, unanimous decision said that "a retention election is not an 'election.'" The court also ruled that, by limiting the election to the incumbent, the legislature had created a new "qualification" for high court candidates, beyond the qualifications in the constitution.

The state supreme court, with its 4-3 conservative majority, accepted the legislature's appeal. When the court took the case, Kromm wrote an op-ed in the News & Observer arguing that Edmunds had to recuse himself. A few days later, he did. The court then deadlocked 3-3, which meant the lower court's decision was upheld.

State courts had thwarted the legislature's plan to tilt the high court election in favor of a conservative incumbent. Voters would have a chance to elect a progressive majority in November 2016.

CHAPTER 12

THE GOP TAKEOVER OF FEDERAL COURTS

Earls spent the night of the 2016 election at home on the couch in her living room. As Trump's lead grew, so did her dread about what his presidency would mean for the courts and voting rights.

Earls spent the evening with her husband, former Rhode Island state Sen. Charles Walton, whom she described as "the most extreme" type of political junkie. In 1983, Walton became Rhode Island's first Black state senator, after election districts were redrawn under the VRA.

The couple tried to comfort one another as the results came in. "I was stunned and ... fearful," Earls said. "It just felt like the world was coming to an end." The implications for the federal courts were clear.

She had been excited about the possibility that President Hillary Clinton would appoint a fifth progressive justice, after the GOP-led U.S. Senate had refused to vote on President Obama's nominee. Earls had recently addressed a group of young Legal Aid lawyers and told them they could, for the first time in their lives, see a majority of Democratic appointees on the High Court. "Courts as an institution are incredibly conservative to begin with," she said. "People do not understand the fact that for 50 years, we've had a Supreme Court controlled by Republican appointees."

After the election, Trump would get to fill the pivotal seat on the Court. In fact, he inherited dozens of empty seats on the federal courts, because the Republican-led U.S. Senate had refused to even consider nominees from President Obama.

Earls recalled, "During the campaign in 2016, Trump was very clear about his focus on the courts and who he was going to nominate." The GOP candidate had been the first major-party nominee to release a list of potential U.S. Supreme Court nominees, and many of them had records of ruling against plaintiffs in voting rights cases.

Earls' courtroom foe, Thomas Farr, would be re-nominated by President Trump to be a federal judge in 2017. Trump's nominees tended to be younger than previous appointees, some in their thirties, but the president made an exception for the 62-year-old Farr.

Farr was nominated to preside over the Eastern District of North Carolina, the Northern tip of the "Black Belt" that extends across the South. Around half of the state's Black population lives in the district, but no Black federal judge had ever served there. For years, Sen. Helms had blocked Black judicial nominees.

Rev. Barber had lobbied for the appointment of a Black federal judge there. President Obama nominated two Black women, but the Republican Senate wouldn't hold a vote on them.

Barber, who lives in eastern North Carolina, said of the district, "when you look at the federal bench, it looks like the civil rights movement never happened." The reverend criticized Farr in moral terms. He said the lawyer has spent his career "at the center of voter suppression." Farr is "genteel," and certainly won't be heard using the n-word, Barber said, "But his commitment to the policies of systemic racism … is chronic and dangerous to the principles of our democracy."

At his confirmation hearing, Farr faced questions about his record of defending voter suppression and his role in crafting the 2013 voter ID law. A senator asked him why legislators had requested data on IDs possessed by African Americans.

Farr argued that lawmakers sought this information to ensure they were complying with the VRA when they drafted the bill. "At the time some of this information was requested, Section 5 was still in place," he testified. "They were going to have to explain how the law didn't have a discriminatory impact." Farr compared the 2013 law to voting rules in other states.

NAACP President Derrick Johnson spoke at a rally in D.C. and argued that any senator supporting Farr was adopting "an anti-democracy agenda." Senators Cory Booker and Kamala Harris, who had become the only Black members of the Senate Judiciary Committee earlier that year, called on their colleagues not to confirm Farr. Echoing Barber, Booker said, "This is a moral moment in our country."

Leslie Proll, a civil rights lawyer who advises the NAACP on judicial nominees, noted that "civil rights cases are a mainstay of North Carolina's federal docket. Even before these plaintiffs walk through the door of Judge Farr's courtroom, they could easily believe their case was doomed."

In the fall of 2017, Farr was approved by the Senate Judiciary Committee on a party-line vote. His nomination would head to the full Senate, where Senate Majority Leader Mitch McConnell was running an assembly line of judicial confirmations.

The federal judiciary's turn to the right would mean fewer victories for voting rights. After Trump's election, Earls felt like she would no longer have an impact in federal court, where they had won the legal battles—so far—against racial gerrymandering and the 2013 voter suppression bill.

Earls realized that state courts would be the key to protecting the rights of voters in North Carolina. And those voters were fortunate that a new progressive majority was elected to their state supreme court in 2016, the same year Trump carried the state.

Republicans were furious. They couldn't accept that the new high court majority threatened their power.

CHAPTER 13

UNDOING THE VOTERS' DECISION

On Election Day 2016, there were silver linings for Democrats in North Carolina. Judge Mike Morgan won election to the North Carolina Supreme Court by double digits, creating a new progressive majority. Voters also elected Gov. Roy Cooper and Attorney General Josh Stein, both Democrats. But Cooper wouldn't be sworn in for several weeks, which meant that the lame-duck governor could sign bills that limited the impact of the voters' decisions.

With Democratic control of the executive and judicial branches, the GOP legislature's power would finally face some checks. Cooper would have the power to veto bills, issue executive orders, and appoint election officials. The gerrymandered Republican legislature could still override the governor's vetoes, but that would require near-unanimous support among their ranks. Any bills they did pass could face challenges at the new high court.

Addressing a crowd of protesters, Barber noted that the 2016 election results showed how far North Carolina had come. Before the election, "because of gerrymandering and other trickery, all three branches of government were in control of extremists who hijacked the Republican Party." But he said, "Last November, y'all … even as Trump-ism swept across the South, extremists in this state lost the executive and the judicial branches. We know how to fight!"

Republicans also knew how to fight, and they would do everything they could to dominate the other branches of government. They had already planned bills to drastically limit the governor's power and un-do the voters' decision to elect a progressive North Carolina Supreme Court.

The state constitution allowed the legislature to add two seats to the court. If lawmakers did that before McCrory left office, his appointments would maintain the court's conservative majority. And the lame duck governor's appointees wouldn't be on the ballot until 2018.

Mitch Kokai of the conservative Carolina Journal discussed the possibility of adding two justices. The headline read, "Legislature could counteract Supreme Court election result by expanding high court."

For the recently victorious Democrats, the news felt like a punch to the gut. The voters chose Morgan, and now the legislature was going to un-do all of it.

Earlier that year, Republican legislatures in two other states—Arizona and Georgia—had engaged in court packing to create new conservative majorities. But even those court-packing schemes didn't blatantly overturn the voters' choice in a recent election.

The scheme to pack North Carolina's highest court was criticized by judges from both parties and editorial boards across the state. Barber and the NAACP threatened to "turn our lawyers loose under … the Voting Rights Act to challenge this power grab." Earls argued that the GOP's plan "would be a highly polit- icized move and do great damage to the court."

Former Justice Orr told NC Policy Watch that his fellow Republicans had discussed the idea months ago, when state courts were weighing the challenge to the law that would've kept Morgan off the ballot. All year long, court packing had been the Republicans' back-up plan if the voters elected a progressive high court majority. And Orr said the power grab was motivated by the desire to preserve their gerrymandered majority.

On December 2, 2016, Gov. McCrory called a "special" session, which would be held two weeks later. It would be the fourth special session of the year. Ostensibly, lawmakers were back in Raleigh to provide funding to recover from a hurricane that had slammed into Eastern North Carolina that fall. They waited until after the election, months after the storm.

Barber said that getting legislators to come back to Raleigh under the auspices of hurricane relief "continues the worst of this extremist legislature's legacy: making unjust laws to give more power to themselves, on the backs of those most vulnerable."

The legislature passed a hurricane relief bill, adjourned, and then immediately convened another special session. Republicans had planned it out but only gave Democrats two hours' notice.

When asked about the agenda, Rep. Lewis cryptically told reporters they would "see the General Assembly look to reassert its constitutional authority in areas that may have been pre- viously delegated to the executive branch." Republican Rep. Jeff Collins argued that his branch of government should be more powerful, because legislators are "the closest state officials to the electorate." But Lewis acknowledged that the power grabs wouldn't be happening if McCrory had been reelected.

During the lame duck session, Republicans passed laws limiting executive power or transferring it to the legislative branch. They took the governor's power to appoint the officials in charge of elections, universities, and the state ethics commission.

New laws would require the state senate to confirm the members of the governor's cabinet. And the attorney general, who had refused to defend H.B. 2 and the voter suppression bill in court, would now have to seek the legislature's permission to withdraw from a lawsuit.

Democratic Sen. Jeff Jackson suggested that Democrats had been set up. He argued that hurricane relief was a false pretense, and he called the lame duck agenda "massively disrespectful to voters." Progressive commentator Rob Schofield of NC Policy Watch called it "a new low in North Carolina politics."

Activists packed the halls of the capitol. Dozens were arrested for interrupting the legislature. Protesters took over the galleys overlooking the floor of the legislature, singing or chanting "You work for us" and "Shame!" Lawmakers closed the galleries to the public and engaged in their power grabs behind closed doors.

The protests were national news. People across the country saw activists arrested for disrupting the legislature. One Black woman appeared to call out to the crowd as the police shackled her. Progressives around the country sounded the alarm bells about the power grabs.

Despite the outcry, the bills were passed by a legislature that had been elected in unconstitutional, racially discriminatory districts. And they were signed into law by the governor that voters had just rejected.

The changes even went too far for some conservatives. Kokai called the lame-duck process "very flawed."

Voting rights advocates were furious about the court packing plot. Kromm said, "Power grabs like this don't give us justice, they give us injustice." She noted that lawmakers weren't talking publicly about their plan. "The M.O. of this Republican legislature has been discussing behind closed doors and passing bills at the last minute," Kromm said.

Kromm had lobbied against the idea and said that some rank-and-file Republicans had opposed it. Gov. McCrory later claimed that he had worked behind the scenes to stop the scheme.

Barber called the lame-duck power grabs "deep violations" of the democratic process. And Rep. Larry Hall, Democratic leader, said simply, "This ain't right…. The people of North Carolina aren't being treated right. We owe them more."

For three days straight, protestors interrupted the legislature with chants and coordinated protests. Commentators and editorial boards decried the power grabs. Prof. Steven Greene at N.C. State University said the actions were particularly alarming in the wake of Trump's election. "People don't realize how much a stable democracy depends on norms, not actually the laws," Greene said, "Just because you can do something doesn't mean you do it."

Jedidiah Purdy of the *New Yorker* said, "There are bedrock principles in a constitutional democracy: that majority wins and constitutional rules, so far as they are clear, are respected. Gerrymandering and voter suppression throw majority rule into question—and changing the rules after an election is not in the spirit of constitutional consistency."

Lawmakers backed down from their most brazen power grab, and the court packing scheme wasn't executed. Hours after the NAACP held a press conference calling them out, Republican leaders told journalists that they never intended to pack the court. But in the coming years, Republicans would occasionally mention the possibility of packing or impeaching the state supreme court, whenever they didn't like its rulings.

Instead of packing the court, the lame-duck legislature created new rules for lawsuits that challenged their legislation. These cases would now be heard by a three-judge panel, instead of judges based in Raleigh. And they could no longer bypass the Court of Appeals, which had a conservative majority.

Republicans introduced a bill making state supreme court races partisan. Though Morgan won in 2016, Republican candidates had swept all three Court of Appeals races, which had already been made partisan by the legislature.

Another bill allowed parties to ask the Court of Appeals to hear the case "en banc," meaning that all 15 judges decide the case, instead of a three-judge panel. The court's conservative majority was narrow, but legislators wanted to take advantage of it.

Earls said in a statement from SCSJ, "Instead of a court-packing bill, it appears we got a court-denial bill. This proposal seems to delay Supreme Court review of cases, including those involving citizens' constitutional rights. Unconstitutional laws could be in effect for years before the state Supreme Court would finally get the case and rule."

The first voting rights battle would come soon, as legislators tried to put their allies in charge of running elections.

CHAPTER 14

FAITHFULLY EXECUTING ELECTION LAWS

One of the GOP's lame-duck laws would have given the legislature, instead of the governor, control over administering elections. The bill and its progeny would face a series of court battles, with Republicans trying again and again to take the power to appoint election officials from the executive branch. During the McCrory administration, his election officials had moved polling places and cut early voting hours, and the bill would allow Republicans to do this again.

On Election Day in 2014, Warren Coleman took a break around 11:30 am from his job in the kitchen at Amelie's, a trendy, upscale bakery/coffee shop that's open 24 hours a day. Coleman, a Black man with a long goatee and glasses, drove 15 minutes from the bakery in the North Davidson (NoDa) neighborhood, crossing under Interstate 77, to his usual polling place at a library in Lincoln Heights.

Coleman walked up to the library's sliding door, still wearing a white apron over his orange sweatshirt, matching his Detroit

Tigers cap. He stopped abruptly at the entrance. Someone had taped a sign on the door letting people know they couldn't vote here. The library had been an early voting site and an Election Day polling place for years. The sign told confused voters where to go.

Election officials had decided to move the polling place at the Lincoln Heights library, even though it had been used for early voting. Before the 2013 voter suppression law, voters could cast their ballot in any precinct in their county.

Dozens of voters, most of them were African American, showed up to vote at the library that morning. Many of them had been voting there for years. Bobbi Parker, an older woman volunteering with the Democratic Party, said some of the voters had disabilities that made it hard for them to get to the polling place. "It was just a terrible situation," she said.

Coleman was lucky. He drove to the new polling place and cast his ballot fairly quickly. It was after noon, and he rushed to get back to work.

Despite the hassle, Coleman was determined to cast his ballot. "Voting is worth it," he said. Other voters weren't so lucky. With less early voting and no out-of-precinct voting in 2014, many urban communities saw long wait times at polling places.

In 2016, local election boards appointed by McCrory slashed the amount of time for early voting, despite a federal court striking down the 2013 voter suppression law, partly because of cuts to early voting. Dallas Woodhouse, head of the state GOP, sent out an email to Republicans, asking them to show up at local election board hearings to speak out against early voting.

The cuts to early voting also seemed to have their intended impact. After the 2016 election, Robin Hayes of the state Republican Party sent out a post-election press release bragging that fewer Black voters had cast their ballots early. Hayes said, "African American early voting is down 8.5% from this time in 2012. Caucasian voters early voting is up 22.5%."

Voter suppression didn't help McCrory keep his job. But before Gov. Cooper took office in 2017, the lame duck legislature passed a law that would have taken away his control of the state elections board. Cooper would have continued to appoint a majority of the board, but only in odd-numbered years. Republicans would appoint the board in even-numbered years, which happen to include state and federal elections.

An elections board aligned with the GOP legislature would open the door to more voter suppression. And the law was just one of many that December that targeted executive power.

The voters had elected a Democratic governor and attorney general, but the gerrymandered Republican legislature passed laws to minimize their power before they took office. They changed hundreds of state jobs from political appointments to career civil servants. McCrory got 1,500 appointments, but Cooper would only appoint 300 people.

Republicans also slashed the attorney general's budget and limited his ability to withdraw from defending laws they had passed. They transferred authority and control from the executive to the legislative branch, even though the constitution requires that those powers be "forever separate and distinct." The separation of powers provision had been part of North Carolina's Constitution since 1776, and Republicans were acting like it didn't exist.

The new elections board law was struck down in 2017, with the court citing this provision and the governor's constitutional responsibility to "faithfully execute" state laws, including election laws.

Republicans responded with a new bill. Instead of alternating control of the board, the legislature created a new elections board, half of which would be chosen by the governor and half by lawmakers. Less than a month later, a judge blocked the law. The case was transferred to a three-judge panel that had been selected by the conservative chief justice, under a law that was also passed during the lame-duck session.

The North Carolina Supreme Court affirmed the ruling to block the law on a 4-3 vote along ideological lines. The court said the governor must have people who share his policy agenda to help him "faithfully execute" state laws, but the legislation required enough Republicans on the board "to block the implementation of the governor's policy preferences."

Lawmakers tried again and again to take control of the election board. The courts kept striking down their bills. One bill would have let the governor appoint the board, but he would have to choose from lists supplied by the two political parties, appointing an equal number of Republicans and Democrats.

In early 2017, the Court of Appeals upheld one of the bills. And the newly-constituted Board of Elections met briefly. But the high court reversed the decision and declared the board unconstitutional. Legislators eventually conceded and created an elections board in which Cooper could appoint a Democratic majority.

When Cooper challenged a law requiring confirmation of his cabinet appointments, a state court put the senate's confirmation hearings on hold. Republican leaders Berger and Moore responded by threatening the court and demanding that it reverse its ruling.

"Their decision to legislate from the bench will have profound consequences, and they should immediately reconvene their panel and reverse their order," Berger and Moore said in a press release. The court defended its authority, but it soon lifted the order blocking the hearings.

CHAPTER 15

SUPERMAJORITY AT RISK

Earls and her colleagues won crucial victories in federal court in advance of the 2018 election. The courts had struck down much of the 2013 voter suppression bill and ordered legislators to redraw districts that discriminated against Black voters. The new districts would give Democrats the chance to end the GOP's veto-proof supermajority.

The legislature's attempts to disenfranchise certain voters were being thwarted by the courts. Federal judges were seeing through Farr's arguments to justify the legislature's voter suppression.

Judge Wynn wrote the decision to strike down the racially gerrymandered congressional districts, and he was on the three-judge panel that affirmed the decision to strike down the wide-ranging voter suppression law in July 2016. The court castigated legislators for seeking out data on voting practices by race and then passing a law that restricted practices used by Black voters.

Rev. Barber told reporters, "We are beyond happy that the Fourth Circuit Court of Appeals exposed for the world to see the racist intent of the extremist element of our government in North

Carolina… The ruling is a people's victory, and it is a victory that sends a message to the nation." (*See Chapter 7.*)

The decision by Judge Diana Gibbons Motz said that Republican lawmakers had targeted Black voters "with almost surgical precision." The phrase echoed throughout the country, because it affirmed the extent to which the voter suppression bill was a Jim Crow-style effort to keep Black people from voting.

The phrase shocked the nation's conscience, but it came almost as an aside during the judges' discussion of the legislature's "voter fraud" justification: "Although the new provisions target African Americans with almost surgical precision, they constitute inapt remedies for the problems assertedly justifying them and, in fact, impose cures for problems that did not exist."

The voter ID and racial gerrymandering decisions were both upheld by the U.S. Supreme Court in the spring of 2017. One month after the Senate confirmed Justice Neil Gorsuch, filling a seat that they had left open for a year, the U.S. Supreme Court declined to review the Fourth Circuit's ruling in the voter ID case.

Cooper and the Democratic Attorney General had withdrawn the state's appeal. Legislators had tried to join the case to defend the law, but the justices seemed exasperated with the issue. In the Court's order, Chief Justice Roberts noted that their decision not to hear an appeal didn't mean they thought the lower court's ruling was correct.

The Court explicitly upheld the rulings to strike down election districts. Earls said the Court confirmed what they had known for years in North Carolina: "The voters of this state are entitled to have fair legislative districts that do not discriminate against voters based on their race."

After federal judges undid their racial gerrymander, Republican legislators saw the writing on the wall. The new districts still discriminated against Democrats, but they were somewhat less gerrymandered. Republicans faced the possibility of losing their supermajority in 2018, and the national political climate made it seem more likely.

Legislators also worried that state courts would require them to fix the election districts that still favored the GOP. It seemed unlikely that the U.S. Supreme Court, reshaped by Trump's appointments, would overturn the districts because of their partisan bias. Earls' organization would try to convince the justices, but they knew it was an uphill battle.

The new progressive majority on the North Carolina Supreme Court, however, was more likely to insist on maps that didn't discriminate against voters of one party.

If Republicans were going to rig the courts to keep that from happening, they had to act before the potential loss of their supermajority in 2018. Cohen, the former legislative attorney who now serves on the board of elections, predicted that Republicans would lose their supermajority "so they're trying to pass as much as they can before December 31."

The power grabs escalated as the election approached. Republicans even had another court packing scheme up their sleeve. Kromm said it was clear the power grabs were motivated by legislators' desire to maintain their gerrymandered districts. "They were doing the math. They were thinking about saving their skins in 2020," she said. They would try—over and over again—to seize control of the judicial branch.

CHAPTER 16

THE GOP VS. THE COURTS

In 2017, Judge Bob Hunter was serving on the North Carolina Court of Appeals. He had been appointed by McCrory, having previously served on the court. And he found himself in the middle of a tug-of-war between the governor and legislature over what would happen to his seat when he retired.

Hunter speaks thoughtfully, and his Southern drawl grows loud enough to command a courtroom. A moderate Republican and a history buff, Hunter is quick to point out examples of power grabs by the long-ruling Democrats in the state legislature. In a recent interview, he said that he doesn't like it when either party makes "racial appeals," which he believes have a "corrosive effect" on politics.

Hunter was born in Greensboro. His mother had been a schoolteacher, and his father worked in construction. Hunter came of age in the 1960s, when four college students launched the sit-in movement for racial integration at a Woolworth's in downtown Greensboro.

He said that he became a Republican partly because he was a contrarian. "Everyone around me was a Democrat," he recalled, and many of them were "smug and arrogant." Hunter read Barry Goldwater's book but found himself drawn to the party's more moderate wing. He also argues that "voters have more choices" now, and "competition is good."

In a 1987 law review article on racial gerrymandering, Hunter outlined the history of how North Carolina became a one-party state after the post-Civil War Reconstruction. The legislature in 1875 had amended the state constitution to ensure "white Democratic control" over majority-Black counties in eastern North Carolina. Legislators appointed officials who disqualified Republican voters.

After advising Republican officials at the Department of Justice on redistricting, Hunter went into private practice. In 1992, when he was serving on the state board of elections, Hunter joined a federal lawsuit that challenged the statewide election of local Superior Court judges.

In 2008, Hunter defeated a Democratic appointee in a race for a seat on the Court of Appeals. He ran for a seat on the high court in 2014, and months before the election, Gov. McCrory appointed him to the seat he was seeking. But Hunter lost to a progressive justice, so McCrory put him back on the Court of Appeals.

A few years later, Republicans passed a law that "unpacked" the N.C. Court of Appeals. Three Republican judges were going to reach the mandatory retirement age in the next couple of years, and one of them was Hunter. The court would lose its narrow GOP majority.

Rather than let the Democratic governor fill the upcoming vacancies, the legislature passed a law shrinking the size of the court by three judges. Republicans suggested, without any evidence, that the court's workload wasn't enough for 15 judges. Duke law professor Marin Levy pointed out the lack of any evidence that the court was overworked. She said the facts suggested that the legislature's goal was to "to keep a sizable majority of the judges on the court Republican."

Cooper vetoed the court unpacking bill, and Republicans planned to override his veto. As that happened, the *News & Observer* in Raleigh reported on an incident months earlier, during the 2016 lame-duck session, that put the lie to any claims about the Court of Appeals' workload. The head of the state GOP had called Judge Doug McCullough, a Republican, and asked him to retire from his seat on the Court of Appeals, so the lame-duck governor could fill his seat with a Republican appointee. The judge refused.

McCullough would retire on his own terms, and he decided to leave the court just before the legislature overrode Cooper's veto of the court unpacking bill. Protesting the bill to shrink his court, McCullough resigned on April 24, 2017 at 9:30 am, allowing Cooper to fill the seat. By 9:45 am, Cooper's appointee, Judge Arrowood, was sworn in. Arrowood would go on to become the first LGBTQ+ official elected statewide.

The legislature's "court unpacking" bill was just the beginning. Lawmakers also made judicial elections partisan. Republicans believed that partisan races would lead to more GOP judges. Barber and the NAACP opposed the move to partisan races.

North Carolina became the first state in almost 100 years to adopt partisan judicial elections. Rep. Marcia Morey, a Democrat who served for decades as a judge, said in the *New York Times*, "I feel like we're taking off the Black robes and we're putting on red and blue robes... And does that really serve the interests of justice?"

In one of their more breathtaking power grabs, legislators introduced a constitutional amendment to shorten every judges' term to just two years. Every judge would be on the ballot in every election. North Carolina judges would have had the shortest terms in the nation, forcing them into the same never-ending campaign that modern legislators face.

Republicans wanted judges who were constantly running for office in partisan elections and raising money from wealthy donors and law firms. An editorial by WRAL in Raleigh charged

Republicans with believing that "justice in North Carolina doesn't need to be blind. It should go to the highest bidder."

Defending the idea of two-year terms, Rep. David Lewis issued a direct threat to the judicial branch. He told judges that if they "act like" legislators, then his amendment would make them "run like one."

Republicans didn't move forward with their brazen attack on judicial independence. Former Justice Bob Orr said there probably wasn't enough support to pass such an amendment, but he was concerned that the proposal was a "punitive threat" to judges. "That's way over the top, so over the top," he said. "I appeal to my fellow Republicans: Let's be the party of good government. Let's not be the party of coercive government."

Republicans also introduced bills that would have given the legislature control over appointing certain judges. The House passed a bill that would have required the governor to fill vacant judicial seats from lists of potential nominees provided by the political party of the outgoing judge.

It passed another bill that limited the governor to appointing someone of the same party to replace judges, U.S. Senators, or prosecutors who leave before the end of their terms. The state supreme court had upheld a similar 1991 law, passed by Democrats, that limited an incoming Republican governor's trial court appointments.

In his book on the Republican legislature, Nichol discussed a "perhaps less notorious" attack on judicial independence. North Carolina imposes a lot of fees on defendants in criminal cases, but judges can waive those fees. The federal and state constitutions often requires them to be waived for indigent defendants, but Nichol said Republican lawmakers "worked steadily to restrain this traditional judicial authority." He said these measures were "aimed at intimidating judges from doing what their jobs demand and, often, from enforcing the constitution."

Judge McCullough said that the power grabs sent a message to judges: "The legislature wants you to rule a certain way... If you rule a certain way, you'll be rewarded. If you don't, you'll be punished."

Activists warned that the legislature was trying to seize all the power of the other branches of government. And the judicial power grabs were designed to protect the legislature's gerrymandered districts. Journalist Barry Yeoman said that each power grab "is a building block in a larger structure designed to maintain Republican power in the face of a demographic threat."

As the power grabs escalated, Kromm found herself spearheading the effort to protect judicial independence. As an advocate for public financing, NCVCE had experience educating the public about the importance of the courts and judicial independence. Kromm carried around a list of crucial state court cases to illustrate the stakes for ordinary citizens.

She said that many of her allies were initially hesitant to use their resources battling the power grabs. "I felt like Chicken Little, screaming that the sky is falling," she said.

But by the fall of 2017, progressives and voters began to get more active in the fight to protect the courts from Republican legislators. Kromm worked with voting rights groups to host dozens of town halls, rallies, and press conferences around the state.

The first town hall was held on Veterans Day in Fayetteville, a city that includes the Fort Bragg military base. When Kromm scheduled the hearing, she hadn't noticed the holiday. She tried to reschedule, but Val Applewhite, a veteran and organizer who now serves on the Fayetteville City Council, told Kromm that "there's nothing more important to do on Veterans Day than defending democracy here at home."

More than 100 people showed up: judges, faith leaders, and concerned citizens. Kromm was elated, but a little nervous to address the bigger crowd. She went on to address crowds across the state. At each event, dozens or hundreds of people gathered to learn about the attacks on their courts. Two hundred people gathered at a town hall in a Greensboro synagogue.

She worked closely with the NAACP and Democracy North Carolina. Rev. T. Anthony Spearman had taken over leadership of the state NAACP, and he denounced the power grabs with the same moral clarity as Barber.

The coalition had its hands full. Lawmakers began to get creative.

CHAPTER 17

GERRYMANDERING
THE JUDGES

At 9:14 pm on Sunday, June 25, 2017, a new redistricting bill was proposed by Rep. Justin Burr, a young, sharply dressed Republican with a shaved head and goatee. Burr, the owner of a bail bond company, announced his plan on social media. "Attached are the maps for … H.B. 717, which will be heard tomorrow at 4:00 pm," @RepJustinBurr tweeted.

Earlier that year, Burr had cosponsored the bills to "unpack" the Court of Appeals, make judicial elections partisan, and give political parties control over judicial appointments. He sponsored a bill in 2016, as protests raged in Charlotte over the police shooting of Keith Lamont Scott, that would have immunized drivers who hit protesters who were blocking traffic.

In March 2017, Burr had proposed a bill to draw judicial election districts in Charlotte. His new bill would redraw districts across the state. Burr argued the districts were overdue for an update, especially in the state's fast-growing cities. He pointed to population disparities in Charlotte's Superior Court districts.

The House Judiciary Committee met on a humid summer morning on June 26, 2017. The room looked like a large conference room, mostly off-white and some wood paneling, with an elevated dais for committee leaders. Lawmakers, who rarely started on time, milled about the rows of desks. The twangs of Southern white men were punctuated with boisterous laughter. Activists who came to speak were either mingling or quietly glaring at lawmakers, anxious to speak their peace and go home or back to work.

Burr eventually came to the podium, standing above his colleagues, and introduced his bill with a resolute, committed tone of voice. Burr talked about his proposal like the matter was already decided, and Republicans said they planned to pass the bill by the end of the week.

The proposal had been unveiled on Sunday evening, and by the end of the week, Republicans planned to redraw judicial election districts across the state. The new districts were displayed for the committee. Burr's bill split up the same cities that had been divided in other redistricting bills.

Democrats accused the GOP of racially gerrymandering the courts. Burr denied it and claimed they were "correcting gerrymandered districts" drawn by previous Democratic legislatures.

When Democrats pressed him on whether his proposal would put more Republicans on the bench, Burr got defensive. "We are fixing problems of the past!" he asserted. Conservative commentators had been arguing for adjustments to the districts, claiming that population disparities made the districts unconstitutional.

Responding to judges' concerns about his bill, Burr accused his critics of protecting their own power. He argued that judges don't like it when others "play in their sandbox." When asked if he had consulted with judges or the court system, Burr said he hadn't: "I'm the legislator. I make the laws."

Democratic Rep. Jean Farmer-Butterfield said the bill was partisan gerrymandering, and judges in her district were angry.

"This weekend, my phone was off the hook. Judges are very upset about this. People in the community are concerned and they feel like they haven't had the chance to have any input," she told the alternative weekly *IndyWeek*.

Another Democrat asked if it was "pure accident" that the new districts seemed to benefit Republican candidates. Rep. Darren Jackson, the minority leader, argued that "different areas of the state are treated differently, for some reason... We're dividing up urban counties that tend to vote Democratic. And we're not dividing up counties that tend to vote Republican."

An analysis from the progressive group Real Facts NC found that Burr's bill would give Republican candidates an advantage. Burr denied gerrymandering the courts, but a legislative aide later told a group of judges that their goal was electing more Republican judges.

Democratic Rep. Joe John, a former judge, pointed out that Black voters were crammed into certain districts. But Burr maintained, "I did not take into account race when redrawing the maps that are before you. It was not a factor in redrawing these districts."

Some lawmakers wanted to break for lunch before public comments, but Burr pressed forward. It seemed like some of the activists were hangry. After years of court battles and revised election districts, Tar Heels understood why gerrymandering was so unfair. And they were furious that Republicans were about to gerrymander their judges.

Kromm was fuming. "You're crippling the courts, punishing the people of North Carolina, just to grease the wheels of partisan politics," she told legislators.

Lekha Shupeck, an anti-gerrymandering activist, called the bill "an effort to push Democratic judges out of office while giving a partisan advantage to Republicans." She pointed out that the proposals put twice as many Democrats in districts with other incumbents.

Diana Wynn from the local League of Women Voters criticized the rushed process and said, "An independent judiciary is a cornerstone of our governmental system of checks and balances." She called for more deliberation and transparency. The state chapter of the League read a statement decrying the unfairness of gerrymandering.

Michael Eisenberg argued the hearing shouldn't be taking place, because the legislature was "unconstitutionally constituted." He referred to a recent federal court ruling that the legislative election districts discriminated against Black voters. He called Burr's bill "an attempted coup d'état."

Eisenberg heard a chuckle and responded, "Rep. Burr, this is not funny." He warned that taking over the courts is "the final piece of the puzzle" for Republicans to keep their supermajority. "The judiciary will become a rubber stamp," he argued. "If this occurs, democracy in North Carolina will officially end."

Several voters criticized the rushed, opaque process and reminded legislators of their duty to their constituents. Shupeck testified, "This court system is the means by which the state delivers justice to its people," and the rushed redistricting process threatened access to justice.

Shupeck said that 40 percent of Democratic Superior Court judges would be double bunked (placed in a district with another incumbent). But only 12 percent of Republican judges were double bunked. Shupeck also argued that the bill disproportionately impacted Black voters.

No one spoke in favor of the bill. But it passed the House committee along party lines, 19 hours after it was released on Twitter. Burr's proposal came near the end of the legislative session, and lawmakers adjourned a week later, with plans to convene again in the fall.

Voters and judges spoke out against the plan and questioned the urgency of redrawing districts before the 2018 election. Former

Republican Justice Bob Orr said, "You just don't draw up a map in the backroom and try and run it through for a vote."

An editorial by WRAL put the redistricting bill in broader context: "It is all part of a plan, reminiscent of the Jim Crow era, to enshrine a narrow ideology and impose their rules."

Douglas Keith of the Brennan Center for Justice, who tracks threats to judicial independence, called for a "more careful approach." Keith said, "Changing court boundaries can have a significant impact on judicial caseloads, allocation of resources, and burdens on clerks and administrators."

Judge Elizabeth Heath, who was president of the N.C. District Court Judges Association, acknowledged that some updates were needed to judicial election districts. But she argued that the process should be transparent and allow input from citizens and judges.

The judicial establishment preferred a different approach outlined in another pending bill, which would have asked the N.C. Courts Commission to study the issue and make recommendations to the legislature.

Burr said the GOP was planning a special session in October 2017 to redraw their own election districts, because federal courts had found that they discriminated against Black voters. (*See chapter 15*.) After fixing those districts, Burr planned to bring up his judicial redistricting bill. That gave organizers and activists time to build opposition.

In the fall, Republicans created a special "judicial reform and redistricting" committee that included members of both houses of the legislature. When they scheduled a vote on Burr's bill, protesters rallied outside the capitol. Many of them had taped over their mouths and written "silenced voter" or other messages on the tape.

Local and national media gave voice to the outrage. A *New*

York Times article commented that the Republican supermajority had seen "a steady stream of laws affecting voting and legislative power rejected by the courts. Now lawmakers have seized on a solution: change the makeup of the courts."

The vote was rescheduled. Burr persisted. He released another version of the maps in December.

Earls said the new districts were similar to legislative election districts that had been struck down as unconstitutional. A 2018 analysis by SCSJ found that Republican judges could be expected to win around 70 percent of the state's local judicial elections in the proposed districts. SCSJ said Burr's bill seemed "clearly intended to rig the judiciary in favor of Republicans."

Of the 26 double-bunked judges, 19 were Democrats. If the maps were enacted, all of those judges would have to leave the bench or run against another Democrat. Rep. Morey, the former judge, said that "judicial redistricting by this legislature is for one purpose only—politics."

The double-bunked judges continued to speak out. At the time, Judge Eula Reid was the only Black judge presiding over a district in the heavily Black northeastern corner of the state, and she warned of the map's impact on judicial diversity. Reid said she served as a role model for young people in her community.

Judge Carl Fox, who is also Black, said, "The percentage of African-Americans in court, regrettably, is probably well over 50 percent, and certainly the numbers in prison represent that, and it's difficult to think that you're going to get any measure of justice when you walk in the courtroom and you never see a face like yours on the bench or in any position of power in that courtroom."

In October 2017, Burr's bill passed the House with one Democrat voting for it. But the Senate didn't schedule a vote on the bill for months.

At legislative hearings, Burr and his Republican colleagues

continued trying to convince Democrats that they weren't gerry-mandering judges. Democrats repeatedly pressed Burr on the criteria used to draw the maps, and Burr insisted they didn't draw them based on race or party.

Judges protested that the new election districts would lead to high turnover on the bench. Melissa Boughton of NC Policy Watch said, "More than 100 judges with thousands of years of combined experience could be wiped from the North Carolina bench by a bail bond agent who has served less than a decade in the General Assembly, and no one really knows why."

The federal courts had found—over and over again—that the legislature had gerrymandered Black communities. But Burr claimed his new bill was simply an attempt to correct population imbalances in judicial districts.

After encountering strong pushback, Burr agreed to slow down and consult with judges. He released different versions of his maps, each one putting fewer judges in districts with other incumbents.

Despite Republicans' veto-proof majority, Burr seemed to have trouble getting enough support among state senators, who introduced their own judicial redistricting bill in early 2018. It was limited to drawing judicial election districts in Charlotte, Raleigh, and a few smaller jurisdictions.

CHAPTER 18

BLACK JUDGES IN THE QUEEN CITY

Burr's proposal would have carved up diverse neighborhoods in the city of Charlotte. Montclaire South, for example, is near South Boulevard, a five-lane thoroughfare with discount stores, Latino markets, and restaurants. There's a drive-through Pollo Campero at the intersection with Archdale Road, an often-crowded road that winds through a dense residential area with steep hills. Montclaire South is an up-and-coming neighborhood, not far from the airport or bustling downtown Charlotte.

The vast majority of the residents there are black or Latino, but the area is slowly gentrifying. The Republican legislature's judicial gerrymandering bill placed this diverse neighborhood in District 26D, where white voters accounted for two-thirds of the population.

District Court judges, who would run in districts for the first time in Charlotte, heard most of the criminal trials and handled some civil matters like child custody or restraining orders. Judge Kimberly Best, who has served on a District Court in Charlotte for more than a decade, said that she has presided over every kind of case.

Best moved to Charlotte, also known as the Queen City, 20 years ago. She defeated an incumbent judge in the 2008 election. As a Black candidate, Best said it was exciting to be on the same ballot as the first Black president. Best won reelection in 2012 and 2016, her first partisan race.

Growing up in Detroit during the 1980s, Best had witnessed the impact of the crack epidemic, gun violence, and the war on drugs. She said, "I noticed a lot of policing. I didn't notice a lot of help for people." People in her family had struggled with addiction. Her brother, like kids in Flint, Michigan today, had suffered from lead poisoning.

Best graduated from Indiana University's law school, and she said that being a judge was always "in the background of my mind … I felt as though I had a unique approach and could make a difference as a judge." She said judges must apply the law, but they must also consider mitigating factors. Best now presides over "Wellness Court," which seeks to get help for people with mental illness. "Justice is not one-size-fits-all," she said.

In 2017, when Republicans began talking about judicial redistricting, Best said that Charlotte's District Court bench was more diverse than it had ever been, in terms of race and gender. In the 2016 election, the county's first partisan judicial race in more than a decade, Black District Court judges had done very well. But Burr's map would have placed some of those judges in districts that were overwhelmingly white.

A Charlotte judge told Republicans that they were proud of their "diverse bench" and lamented that the city was "being split for partisan purposes."

When other local judges heard about Burr's bill, Best said many of them were "quite afraid" of the legislature. "I knew exactly what they were doing," she said in a recent interview. Best suggested to her fellow judges that they shouldn't negotiate with Republicans over the bill.

In addition to threatening judicial diversity, Best also worried that Republicans would target younger Democratic judges and try to put more Republicans on the bench, setting them up for future appointments to federal courts.

It was also clear that Republicans wanted judges in place who wouldn't let the constitution stand in their way of their agenda. Best said, "If you have the right judges in place, you can … pretty much guarantee that the legislation you pass won't be overturned."

Best wasn't double bunked in Burr's House bill, but after she spoke out, the map introduced in the state Senate eliminated her seat. A friend called her very early one morning and woke her up to tell her the news. She was outraged.

Senators had drawn her into district 26A, which included a wide swath of southern Mecklenburg County, a conservative area along the border with South Carolina. The smaller portion of the district wound from downtown Charlotte through the suburbs, growing very narrow at certain points, to the bulk of the district along the eastern edge of Mecklenburg County, which included Best's home in the suburb of Mint Hill.

The meandering district was 82 percent white. It narrowed when passing through diverse neighborhoods, then reached out to swallow whiter suburbs.

To continue serving, Best would likely have had to move from her home in Mint Hill. And there was "no way that could happen" at that point in her life, she said. Best began thinking about other career options "just in case."

Republicans' argument about population disparities often focused on the Superior Court districts in Mecklenburg County, which includes Charlotte. But for some reason, the redistricting bill also drew election districts, for the first time, for District Court judges like Best.

A Republican who represented a Charlotte-area district argued that voters were "infinitely more likely" to "learn who they want to vote for" when there are fewer candidates to choose from. But critics of Burr's bill pointed out that the judges would continue to preside over the entire county, not just their district.

Creating districts in Charlotte, as well as redrawing districts in Raleigh, helped Republican judicial candidates. An anonymous court official told one reporter that it was "virtually impossible for a Republican to win a countywide judicial election" in Charlotte.

Black judges and legislators warned of the impact of the judicial redistricting bills on racial diversity in other parts of the state. Burr's first bill would have placed more than half of the Black District Court judges in districts with other incumbents.

The lawmakers carved up judicial elections in the same cities they had targeted in the legislative and congressional maps. An analysis by NC Policy Watch illustrated the impact on diverse judges. One of the state's two Latino District Court judges were "double-bunked," as was one of the two Native American Superior Court judges.

For one version of Burr's Bill, SCSJ analyzed the impact on Black and Latino voters in Guilford County, which included the repeatedly gerrymandered city of Greensboro. Voters of color were packed into three districts, and the other two districts were overwhelmingly white.

Democrats had asked Burr repeatedly how he knew the maps complied with the Voting Rights Act. Burr simply responded that they did. He claimed that unless a judge is "legislating from the bench," the maps wouldn't be thrown out as unconstitutional.

Burr repeatedly denied that he was gerrymandering the courts on the basis of race or political party. But in 2019, evidence emerged showing that Burr had turned to Republican gerrymandering expert Thomas Hofeller to draw the districts. Hofeller's hard drive included drafts of the judicial election districts with voters sorted on racial and political lines. Burr had denied working with any experts or consultants during the September 27 hearing.

For months, Burr had also denied knowledge of the impact of his proposals on Black incumbent judges. But his final state-wide map included data on the impact on incumbents. Compared to previous drafts, the map put even more Black Superior Court judges in districts with other incumbents. Burr was finally acknowledging the impact on Black judges, and at the same time, he put more of them in danger of losing their seats.

Republicans had called a special session for May 15, 2018, and Democrats showed up that morning with no idea what was on the agenda. There were rumors that Republicans could propose several constitutional amendments. Everyone assumed they would continue gerrymandering judges.

Like Burr, state senators had revised their proposed districts, responding to some requests from Black judges who had been double bunked or had their seats eliminated. At that point, Burr had released nine different versions of his proposal over the course of a year.

Days earlier, North Carolina had held its May 2018 primary election, and Burr had been defeated by a Republican primary challenger. Legislators speculated about how this would impact his judicial redistricting bill. Sen. Blue, the Democratic leader, said, "I would think that Republicans' push to rig the courts will die down, but anything is possible."

Burr's statewide proposals didn't pass the senate, which had its own bill that redrew districts in Charlotte, Raleigh, and smaller communities. The House passed the Senate bill. Representatives Lewis and Burr were disappointed at the scaled-down final product.

Judge Hunter said that he had conferred with his fellow Republicans and told them their bill was "wrong" and unconstitutional. "I told them not to do it," Hunter said in an interview. Cooper argued the legislature's "piecemeal attempts to target judges show contempt for the North Carolina judiciary."

Charlotte's District Court elections were in for a big change. Four of Charlotte's new districts were majority-white, three of them by more than 70 percent, and the other four districts were more than two-thirds Black.

In countywide elections in 2016, candidates supported by Black voters had won all of the contested District Court elections. But in 2018, two Black judges and six white judges were elected. Four Republican judges were elected in Charlotte, despite the GOP losing countywide elections.

Judge Donald Cureton, a Black Democrat, was narrowly defeated by a less qualified candidate who said that she had run against him because the district was so favorable to Republicans. Judge Alicia Brooks lost to a former prosecutor. Burr's map had placed both Black judges in a district that was 83 percent white.

An official with the state court system had told a reporter that Burr's bill would lead to fewer Black judges and fewer Democrats on the bench in Charlotte. That's exactly what happened. If Burr's statewide proposals had passed, Black judges in cities across the state—Asheville, Greensboro, Fayetteville, and others—would likely have suffered the same fate.

CHAPTER 19

RALLYING FOR
THE COURTS

Barber's movement rallied in Raleigh to protect the courts in January 2018. The reverend started by saying that it's not about right and left. "Some things are about right and wrong," the preacher said. "Woe unto those who legislate evil and rob the poor of their rights." People in the audience were moved to tears. Barber told the crowd, "We march because all of God's creation is important, regardless of race or creed or color or who you choose to love."

North Carolinians rallied outside the capitol on January 10, carrying signs that demanded judicial independence and voting rights. Many of them had printed brown signs that simply read FAIR COURTS NOW. Democracy North Carolina had a table offering signs for those who didn't have one. They had a poster that read "Don't hate. Let the people participate," bordered by pieces of black tape with "silenced voter" written on them, memorabilia from previous protests.

Rev. Spearman of the state NAACP told the crowd they were

here to confront the "unconstitutional, Jim Crow" legislature. Spearman, wearing a purple hat and a purple scarf circling his clerical collar, called Republican legislators "usurpers," who had been elected in illegal districts.

Kromm called on the crowd to tell their legislators to stop the power grabs. "The courts belong to we the people!" Kromm warned other states that "North Carolina is a test case, y'all." If legislators succeed in "stacking, packing and cracking our courts, it will spread like a disease across this country." The parent of a toddler, Kromm compared the legislature's power grabs to her daughter pulling ornaments off the Christmas tree and yelling "mine!"

Kromm and other organizers had worked hard to turn people out. "It was a really good example of being able to pull all of the progressive groups together for a common goal," she said. The rally included groups like the N.C. Council of Churches, environmental groups, labor activists, and so many others.

The protesters heard from Justice Patricia Timmons-Goodson, the first Black woman to serve on the North Carolina Supreme Court. She had been nominated to the same federal judgeship as Farr in Eastern North Carolina, but the Republican-led U.S. Senate refused to hold a vote on her confirmation. At the 2018 rally, Timmons-Goodson called an independent judiciary a crucial part of "the interlocking framework of principles that are in place for our nation to ensure liberty. Judges must be free to enforce the law without fear of reprisal. Otherwise, the other principles and goals of a free society can easily become empty promises."

That fall, opposition to the GOP's judicial agenda in Washington, D.C. was also facing more resistance than ever before. The same voting rights advocates that fought the legislature's power grabs were relentless in their opposition to Farr's nomination to a judgeship in Eastern North Carolina. Farr had spent decades defending

North Carolina Republicans accused of discriminating against Black voters, and President Trump wanted him confirmed to a lifetime seat on the federal judiciary.

Barber, who was denied his request to speak at Farr's confirmation hearing, warned Senators about the lawyer's record in speeches, media interviews, and op-eds. "I have spent my whole life in North Carolina, and I know this nominee," Barber wrote. "I know what he's done, what he stands for, and just how detrimental he will be to the people of North Carolina and this nation if confirmed."

People across the country protested the nomination. U.S. Rep. Marcia Fudge, an Ohio Democrat, denounced Farr at an event in Cleveland on the 50th anniversary of Martin Luther King's death. She said Farr "believes in dirty tricks that we have seen across the South for many, many years and has defended them in court."

It seemed the pressure was working. Farr's nomination languished throughout the summer and fall of 2018.

Across the country, protesters rallied in August 2018 to oppose the nomination of then-Judge Brett Kavanaugh to the U.S. Supreme Court. In D.C., dozens of people were arrested by Capitol Police. Kavanaugh was accused of assaulting a woman as a teen, in addition to other questions about his background.

In September, protesters gathered in Raleigh outside a federal building that housed a courtroom and the office of Sen. Thom Tillis, former legislative leader. A group called "Tuesdays with Tillis" held regular protests there, and this one focused on the federal courts and Kavanaugh.

They were calling on Tillis and other Senators to vote against confirming Farr and Kavanaugh to lifetime seats on federal courts. Two protesters held signs that said, "No SCOTUS for the criminal POTUS." Another sign told Tillis to "Say naw to Kavanaugh." Some of the "raging grannies," dressed in their trademark pink outfits, spoke out against the rush to confirm a judge credibly accused of sexual assault.

The head of the local NAACP, Rev. Dr. Portia Rochelle, warned that confirming Kavanaugh "will result in massive civil rights rollbacks." She quoted NAACP President Derrick Johnson, who had argued that the U.S. Supreme Court could roll back the civil rights victories of the last 50 years. "Everything will be on the table... equal opportunities for college admissions, voting rights, reproductive rights, health care, and other rights that affect our daily living," she said.

Kavanaugh and Gorsuch, another Trump appointee, were the first two justices to be confirmed by senators who represented less than half of the U.S. population. Rev. Barber pointed out, "If we look at George Bush and now Donald Trump, we are poised to have two presidents that did not win the popular vote who will have appointed four members to the Supreme Court, four extreme members to the Supreme Court. We already have a Supreme Court that rolled back the Voting Rights Act. Kavanaugh, we believe, will be dangerous to voting rights."

Kavanaugh was confirmed, after he raged at senators during his confirmation hearing. Republican senators, as well as one Democrat, voted to put Kavanaugh on the Court, despite the testimony from his alleged victim and questions about whether Kavanaugh had lied to them. All that mattered to Republican senators was getting another justice on the bench who conformed to their political agenda.

The GOP was transforming the courts, but Earls continued to demand that federal judges protect the rights of North Carolina voters.

CHAPTER 20

A SHORT-LIVED VICTORY

Earls had brought another gerrymandering lawsuit in 2016. This time, she argued that the legislature's blatant partisan gerrymandering violated the U.S. Constitution. Republicans had admitted that their districts favored their party, and Earls hoped this would persuade judges to do something about extreme gerrymandering.

Rep. David Lewis had stood before reporters and bragged about skewing election districts in the GOP's favor, and he said it was "not against the law." At the time, the U.S. Supreme Court had agreed that partisan gerrymandering could violate the Constitution, but they couldn't agree on how to decide how much is too much.

Earls argued the districts were "by any measure one of the worst partisan gerrymanders in modern American history." She noted that, as Lewis predicted, Republicans would win 10 of 13 Congressional seats, "even if the largest Democratic wave in a generation occurs."

In October 2017, Earls appeared before two three-judge panels to argue redistricting cases. And both panels included Judge

Wynn. Her partisan gerrymandering case had been merged with one filed by Common Cause North Carolina.

On the first day of the trial, Earls and her cocounsel had to throw out their game plan. The judges said they didn't want to hear from lay witnesses, and Earls had planned to have several voters testify. "It was quite a scramble" to focus solely on the experts, she said.

Earls relied on expert analysis from statistician Jowei Chen and others. The briefs filed with the court had laid out how, under three different measures, the GOP's election districts showed enormous "partisan asymmetry."

The Republicans' lawyer pointed out that the U.S. Supreme Court had rejected partisan gerrymandering claims. He argued the plaintiffs had "fallen woefully short" in offering a manageable test and warned that ruling for them "would result in most redistricting done by federal judges."

Earls argued the obviously gerrymandered districts violated the First Amendment and the Equal Protection clause by discriminating against Democratic candidates. She said that extreme gerrymandering is "contrary to core democratic values," because a party can win fewer votes and still gain power. "By sharply distorting the relationship between votes and seats, it causes policies to be enacted that do not accurately reflect the public will," Earls argued in a brief.

Republican legislators accused the plaintiffs of seeking a Democratic advantage. But Earls denied that they aimed "to replace a pro-Republican gerrymander with a Democratic one." They only wanted a map that didn't give either side an unfair advantage.

Earls said in an interview that when Republicans could no longer use race to draw districts, the legislature "interpreted the U.S. Supreme Court as having said it's fine to take into account partisanship." She said the revised maps illustrated the limits of the federal courts' racial gerrymandering rulings, because "discriminating against voters for any reason harms democracy."

The court agreed with Earls, citing Lewis' stated goal of drawing a partisan gerrymander. Wynn wrote the decision, which said that "partisan gerrymandering runs contrary to both the structure of the republican form of government embodied in the Constitution and fundamental individual rights preserved by the Bill of Rights."

The court said that gerrymandering also "insulates representatives from having to respond to the popular will." Wynn noted, "As James Madison warned, a legislature that is itself insulated by virtue of an invidious gerrymander can enact additional legislation to restrict voting rights and thereby further cement its unjustified control of the organs of both state and federal government."

Bob Phillips of Common Cause North Carolina, a plaintiff in the case, called it a victory for voters. "At long last, politicians will no longer be allowed to use partisan gerrymandering in order to shield themselves from accountability to the public," he said.

Republican lawmakers appealed to the U.S. Supreme Court, which had punted on a gerrymandering case out of Wisconsin in 2017. Earls had filed her lawsuit before the 2016 election, when the Court included only eight justices, but now, it had a five-justice conservative majority again. "I tried to be optimistic," Earls said in an interview.

When her case got to the Court, it was combined with one from Maryland, challenging districts drawn by Democrats. Earls hoped that a case involving gerrymandering by both parties would convince the justices to step in. In 2018, the Court sent the case back to the lower court.

Months later, the Court heard arguments, and Earls' protege, Allison Riggs, represented the plaintiffs. The conservative justices, including the two Trump appointees, were skeptical of her argument. Justice Kavanaugh asked Riggs whether Congress or states could solve the problem of extreme gerrymandering.

Riggs responded that citizens couldn't solve the problem in North Carolina, where only the legislature can place amendments or referenda on the ballot. Kavanaugh said, "I'm thinking more nationally." And Riggs responded that those options "don't relieve this Court of its duty to vindicate constitutional rights."

Chief Justice Roberts also seemed to suggest the problem would be solved without the Court's intervention. He worried about federal courts intervening in political disputes. But Riggs pressed her point: "The reputational risk to the Court of doing something is much, much less than the reputational risk of doing nothing, which will be read as a green light for this kind of discriminatory rhetoric and manipulation in redistricting from here on out."

After watching the conservative justices question Riggs, Earls was discouraged. "They had already written their opinion," she said. The court would ultimately throw out the case for the same reason it had thrown out earlier lawsuits challenging partisan gerrymandering.

The Court would continue its trend of limiting the reach of the VRA and other civil rights laws. Voters in North Carolina would have to look elsewhere to protect their rights. Earls had a new plan to help them.

CHAPTER 21

FOR JUSTICE

In November 2017, Earls announced that she was running for the North Carolina Supreme Court against a Republican incumbent. Despite her victories in court, it was clear that Republicans in Washington D.C. were transforming the federal judiciary with Trump's nominees. So, Earls asked herself, "How do I have an impact in state court?"

She thought serving as a judge would be "the best way to protect the rights of communities that traditionally have been disenfranchised." It wasn't the first time she had thought about this career move. In 2010, Earls had been considered by President Obama for a vacant seat in Eastern North Carolina.

Earls thought her experience would be a great asset as a judge. "It's really stunning how few civil rights lawyers are on the bench," Earls said. "Obama didn't appoint many. When it came to appointments, he was actually kind of conservative."

She argued that elections were the only path to the bench for her. "I wouldn't have had a chance to be on the court otherwise. I was able to make my case to the voters." She started by setting up a campaign committee, Anita Earls for Justice. The campaign would mostly rely on small donations, people chipping in small amounts to help out when they could.

Her experience as a lawyer, as well as the time she had spent talking to voters and communities, meant that she was a great speaker. Earls could talk at length about justice and fairness. Her intelligence and empathy were clear to anyone watching her. When fielding questions, she had a very deliberate and thoughtful way of speaking. It was reassuring in a judicial candidate.

Earls, however, wasn't entirely comfortable with talking about herself on the campaign trail. "It took a lot of convincing, from a wide range of consultants, to get me to talk about myself," she said. "The voters want to know who you are."

It wasn't a typical judicial election. Earls campaigned as an unabashed advocate for justice and a critic of the legislature's power grabs. She warned that judicial independence and voting rights were under attack. In her stump speech, Earls listed five ways that Republicans had tried to undermine her campaign. She argued that her victory would illustrate "the importance of an impartial and independent judiciary."

The candidate criticized the state supreme court's rulings to uphold the legislature's racially gerrymandered districts. "Their rulings on the 2011 redistricting plan were twice struck down by the [U.S.] Supreme Court," she said.

Earls highlighted her 30-year record of fighting for the rights of poor and marginalized people. She said this experience taught her the importance of a judiciary that is fair to everyone, not just the wealthy and powerful.

The civil rights community rallied behind her. Derrick Smith of the state NAACP said, "She's been the rock star on the legal front when it comes to voting rights here in North Carolina... Almost every facet, she's been the lead, and we keep winning." She drew a "superstar's welcome" at a campaign stop in Hillsborough, according to journalist Barry Yeoman.

For Republicans, "the prospect of losing a state supreme court seat to their courtroom nemesis has proven particularly distressing," Yeoman said, and they "accelerated their attempts to change how judges are chosen."

CHAPTER 22

ENDING JUDICIAL ELECTIONS

On the same day as Earls' announcement, a joint house/senate committee met for the first time to discuss bills that would change how judges are chosen. Senate leader Berger had announced the committee, months after discussing the possibility of ending judicial elections and moving to an appointment system.

Everyone assumed that Republicans' proposal would give them power over choosing judges. North Carolina's neighbors, Virginia and South Carolina, are the only states where judges are picked by the legislature. In both states, the process has led to charges of corruption and nepotism. A conservative think tank said, "What this means, in effect, is that by the time a judicial nominee becomes a judge in South Carolina, he or she is personally and professionally beholden to state lawmakers in unhealthy ways."

An anonymous North Carolina judge said that a GOP legislative aide had told him that Berger would prefer a system like Virginia's, because legislators don't trust lawyers or judges. The proposals discussed in the legislative hearing didn't go that far. But all of them would have given the legislature itself a bigger role in choosing judges.

Until the post-Civil War Reconstruction era, North Carolina judges had been chosen by the legislature. But the 1868 North Carolina constitutional convention had rewritten the state's fundamental law. Under the protection of Union troops, the convention included men who had been enslaved a few years earlier. Their new constitution included the rights to get an education and vote in "free" elections.

The 1868 convention had also ended the system of letting legislators choose judges. Abraham Galloway, a delegate who had been enslaved, described the judiciary chosen by the Confederate legislature as a "bastard born of sin and secession." Under the new constitution, voters would choose judges in elections that were now open to Black men. And the governor would fill any vacancies that arose.

Exactly 150 years later, the all-white Republican majority in the North Carolina legislature were planning to return some control over choosing judges to the legislative branch.

When Democratic legislators showed up for a Senate committee hearing on January 4, 2018, they weren't sure what bills or amendments would be considered. Republicans at the hearing discussed an amendment that would set up a commission appointed by Chief Justice Martin, a Republican, to narrow down potential appointees to fill vacant judicial seats.

Republicans described the amendment as a "merit selection" reform. But in true merit selection systems, an independent commission composes a list of the most qualified applicants for vacant seats, and the governor chooses from the list.

Under the North Carolina amendment, however, the commission would merely weed out the unqualified judges. Legislators would then be in charge of coming up with a list of two or three applicants, and the governor would have to choose someone from their list to fill a vacant seat.

Editorials across the state criticized the amendment. Ned Barnette of the *News & Observer* said that politicians' "effort to politicize the judiciary is even more brazen" than Republicans in Washington, D.C. The legitimacy of judges "rests on a delicate public perception of judicial independence," Barnette wrote.

The proposal was blasted by current and former judges. State Rep. Joe John (D-Wake), who had served as a judge for twenty-five years, warned that "Republicans seek to rip the blindfold of impartiality from Lady Justice." Former Judge Donald Stephens said the GOP's proposal was not a true merit selection system and warned that it would be "a disaster."

In December, Democrats walked out of a legislative hearing to protest Republicans' decision to keep Stephens from testifying. Stephens planned to testify that the amendment was "a pure and simple power grab to exercise complete control over two branches of government." Stephens and others warned that the proposal would open the door to another court packing scheme.

If Earls lost her election and the amendment passed, the legislature could add two seats to the court and control the process of filling the two vacant seats. This would create a new conservative majority and protect the legislature's gerrymandered districts from state courts.

Rep. Jackson, the Democratic leader, proposed a change to the amendment that would exclude newly created seats from the new appointment process. Republicans voted the proposal down. When Jackson flat out asked Republicans if their goal was court packing, they wouldn't answer. Lewis defended the proposal as an attempt to improve how judges are chosen.

Sen. Floyd McKissick, a Durham Democrat, said that "this whole merit selection process is completely devoid of merit… It was a political grab from the outset."

Lawmakers on both sides of the aisle raised questions about whether the legislature should pick judges. Republican John Blust asked, "Why do we want to take on one more thing that may not be an area we have expertise in?" He also noted that power is concentrated in the hands of legislative leaders. "A few people hold most of the cards, and ... they can bring so much power to sway," Blust said.

At a June 2018 hearing, Republicans hung a flyer on the walls titled "when governors ignore the will of the people." It included pictures and names of judges who were appointed after losing reelection. The flyer didn't mention that many of the judges had been reelected since their appointment.

Democrats were irate. Sen. Terry Van Duyn, from the mountain city of Asheville, angrily accused the GOP of "maligning the character of judges who are not here to defend themselves." Sen. McKissick, one of the longest serving legislators, said he had never seen anything like this. "We ought not be walking down this path," he said.

Rep. Burr defended the effort to give legislators control over filling vacant seats. "Currently, many of these vacancies are filled in secret behind the iron fence of the Governor's mansion with no involvement from the public whatsoever, and I have had a problem with that for years," he said.

In typical fashion, Republicans rolled out a constitutional amendment that Democrats were expected to read in minutes, before casting their votes. The language of the amendment hadn't been shared with all legislators, and it certainly hadn't been shared with the public.

Legislative staff brought in big stacks of papers, stapled copies of the Republicans' proposed constitutional amendment. They sat the stack of papers on one table, leaving activists and journalists to scramble over each other to grab copies.

In Republicans' first draft amendment in 2017, half of the

commissioners would have been chosen by the legislature and half by the governor, in addition to one appointment by the chief justice. But the 2018 proposal didn't specify how many commissioners would be chosen by the legislature. In other words, the original version spelled out how many members would be chosen by each branch of government, but the new proposal left that out.

If the amendment passed, legislators could set up a commission in which they chose all but two of the commissioners, leaving the governor and chief justice with one pick each.

When a Democratic senator pointed out the omission, Republican Sen. Paul Newton feigned surprise. Legislators then voted to change the amendment, but they would still have the ability to appoint a majority of the commission.

Douglas Keith of the Brennan Center for Justice, an advocate for judicial independence, pointed out another difference from the 2017 draft. The original version charged the commission with choosing the "most qualified" applicants for vacant seats, but the new bill said the commission only had to come up with a list of "qualified" applicants. Keith had referred to an earlier, similar proposal as "window dressing on a legislative appointment system."

The amendment would allow the commissioners to choose anyone, as long as they met the minimum qualifications, and the governor would have to choose from their list.

Republicans passed the amendment. It would be on the ballot in November 2018. All six of North Carolina's former chief justices—four Democrats and two Republicans—publicly opposed the amendment. They described the proposed system as "partisan, and not merit-based."

As voters weighed the amendment, Kromm held even more rallies and town halls across the state to educate voters. "I was driving all across the state, lugging around a podium" for press conferences at local courts. She said that people understood the fundamental unfairness of letting the legislature run roughshod over the other branches of government.

Kromm agreed that the power grabs were all about gerrymandering and control of the state supreme court. "They were doing the math. They were thinking about saving their skins in 2020," she said.

She was joined by Sailor Jones from Democracy NC and allies from the NAACP and other civil rights groups. They rallied a small crowd at Gethsemane Baptist Church in Alamance County, a community experiencing deep racial division. The small, diverse crowd was fired up. "In the end, it's up to you," Kromm told them, "You're the ones that decide whether to amend the constitution and give them the power they want."

CHAPTER 23

MISLEADING THE VOTERS

In the summer of 2018, Republicans passed a constitutional amendment giving the legislature control over choosing certain judges. It would be up to the voters to decide whether to ratify it. The legislature wanted to make sure they did. But the Constitutional Amendments Publication Commission, which included two Democrats and one Republican, would write the language on the ballot for the November election. Legislative leaders didn't like that and tried to change it.

Rep. Lewis, the lead gerrymanderer, called a one-day special session so lawmakers could write the ballot language themselves. He claimed, with no evidence, that progressives had pressured the Commission to describe the amendments in a negative way. Lewis cited "maneuverings by interested political outside groups."

Lawmakers convened on July 24, unveiled the new law, and passed it on party lines that evening. They also changed their rules to allow them to more quickly override the governor's veto.

With protesters railing against the changes outside the

building, legislators passed new ballot language. The ballot wouldn't even mention the legislature's role in choosing judges. And it made the amendment seem like a reform.

The vague ballot language was challenged in state court. And the lawsuit prompted Woodhouse, the head of the state GOP, to talk about legislators impeaching judges if they ordered new ballot language.

Woodhouse's threat was not an idle one. Republican legislators had enough votes to impeach judges. And in two states that year, Pennsylvania and West Virginia, GOP-controlled legislatures had introduced bills to impeach all or some of their high court justices.

Despite this threat, state judges ordered new ballot language that didn't mislead voters. The judges found that the legislature's language wouldn't allow voters to "intelligently" decide. Lawmakers then clarified the language describing the amendment.

The court also ordered new ballot language to describe another amendment, which would have given lawmakers control of every state government board and commission. Its description on the ballot was even more misleading.

The ballot wouldn't have mentioned that the amendment radically changed the state constitution's separation of powers provision that had been in place since 1776. It would only tell voters that the amendment would "clarify the appointment authority" of the legislature.

"It's not a clarification. It's an entire rewrite of state government," said Rep. Pricey Harrison, a Democrat from Greensboro. Environmental advocates warned against giving the legislature control over enforcing clean air and clean water regulations. Legislators had long explored the idea of defunding environmental agencies. Derb Carter of the Southern Environmental Law Center described the amendment as "a raw power grab on the part of a legislature that knows and expects they're going to lose their supermajority, and this is their last chance to shoot for the moon."

Five former North Carolina governors, from both parties, publicly opposed both the separation of powers and judicial selection amendments. Former Republican Gov. Jim Martin said, "It's about power politics, and it must be stopped." Martin had seen his authority stripped by a Democratic legislature in the 1980s.

Gov. McCrory even called the ballot measures "deceitful" and "a blatant power grab." When he was in office, McCrory had battled the legislature in court over appointments to a state board that regulated pollution from coal power plants.

WRAL, a Raleigh television station, said Republican leaders had "hastily concocted these amendments in secret, did all they could to make sure there was as little public notice and discussion as possible and worked hard to obscure any details on the impact of these amendments so citizens wouldn't be fully informed when they faced them in the voting booth."

North Carolina's governor was already one of the weakest chief executives in the country. And legislators wanted to take away his power to appoint agency officials. The *Winston-Salem Journal* commented that "there would be little of substance left for the governor to do."

Rather than clarify the extent of their power grab, as the court ordered, lawmakers dramatically scaled the amendment back. The new separation of powers amendment only applied to the elections board.

The amendment would overturn the court rulings to strike down the laws taking away the governor's control over election administration. Before the 2016 election, when the legislature's cuts to early voting had been blocked by a federal court, local Republican election officials were strongly encouraged to cut early voting in their counties. Woodhouse told them, "Our folks are angry and opposed to Sunday voting." If the amendment passed, Republicans would again oversee elections.

After Cooper won, Republican legislators tried repeatedly to take the power to appoint election officials for themselves. (*See chapter 14.*) They lost in court, but the amendment would overturn those rulings and give them the control they sought.

The amendment would establish a four-person board, split evenly between Democrats and Republicans. It was modeled on the Federal Elections Commission, which had been paralyzed by inaction and gridlock for years.

During the special session, an exasperated Rep. Jackson asked Republicans whether an evenly divided board would be more likely to deadlock with tied votes than a board with an odd number of members. "No," responded GOP Rep. John Torbett. Jackson threw up his hand in a shrug and sat down.

Immediately after its one-day special session to rewrite the amendments, lawmakers called yet another special session to make another change to the ballot. The change was intended, according to one Republican lawmaker, to keep Earls off the state supreme court.

CHAPTER 24

MANIPULATING
THE BALLOTS

In July 2018, the legislature passed two separate laws that ensured Earls' name would appear at the very bottom of the ballot in November. The first law moved the high court race to the bottom of the ballot. The second put Earls' name below her opponent. And Republicans weren't even done changing the ballot.

The GOP also attacked Earls in the media. Woodhouse criticized her work representing victims of police harassment. He called her "a danger to human life," and a GOP-linked group attacked Earls in a postcard that included a darkened image of her with a client, a tattooed former gang leader.

Republican legislators cancelled that year's primary elections for judges, even though they had just made those races partisan. Since the incumbent was a Republican, it was plausible that multiple Democrats would enter the race, splitting Earls' support.

Earls said that her focus was on "coming out of the gate strong, so there wouldn't be any other Democrats in the race. My biggest fear was that four or five Democrats would file to run against one Republican." Soon after the primaries were cancelled, a dark money group linked to the state GOP mailed flyers to Democratic lawyers, recruiting them to run for a seat on the supreme court.

The scheme backfired when Republican Chris Anglin filed to run in the general election. Like Earls, Anglin criticized the legislature's attempts to control the judicial branch. A registered Democrat until recently, Anglin said he wanted to offer Republican voters a candidate who believed in the separation of powers. Justice Jackson, the incumbent, responded by calling herself the only true Republican in the race.

Republicans then tried to kick Anglin off the ballot. They passed a retroactive law that said a candidate had to be a member of a political party for 90 days to run as a candidate of that party. The law was passed just hours after it was introduced, and Republicans again changed their rules to more quickly override the governor's veto.

One lawmaker admitted the law was intended to keep Earls off the court. He described her as "to the left of Hubert Humphrey," the former Minnesota senator. Justice Jackson said she wasn't involved with the law.

Earls had known something like this could happen when she signed up to run. She said, "I knew the legislature could try to muck around with the race, but ... I tried to focus on things I could control."

Anglin filed a lawsuit in early August. He said, "Even children understand changing the rules in the middle of an election is wrong." A few days later, the court struck down the law and put Anglin back on the ballot.

Just as they had done in 2015, state courts struck down a law that would have helped keep a Republican justice on the high court. Rep. Lewis described the decision as disappointing and said it would result in "misleading information" for voters.

Nichol's book describes the "constantly shifting rules and constantly moving goalposts" for the 2018 judicial elections, all of which were designed to help elect Republican candidates.

CHAPTER 25

EVERYTHING ON THE LINE

North Carolina's democracy was at stake on Election Day in 2018. At a campaign stop in the mountain town of Hendersonville, Earls said, "I don't think it's an exaggeration to say that our democracy is in peril right now."

She argued that the amendment giving lawmakers control over choosing judges was a first step toward ending judicial elections altogether. "They spend all their time figuring out how to stay in power," Earls said.

The candidate told NC Policy Watch, "We are at a critical moment in our state and nation's history. Our basic civil rights and values are being threatened. Politicians at every level are attacking the independence of our courts in order to maintain their power." Earls warned, "We cannot allow the independence of our courts to be threatened in favor of entrenching the power of a privileged few."

Republican legislators' attacks on voting rights and judicial independence culminated in 2018 with their attempts to rewrite the state constitution, put Republicans in charge of running elections, and open the door to another court packing scheme.

Editorial boards across the state endorsed Earls and urged voters to reject the legislature's power grabs. One editorial called the legislature's amendment "another escalation in an increasingly bitter—and disturbing—fight across the United States to control the judiciary." Some media outlets endorsed Earls and said that electing her would protect judicial independence.

Republicans were trying every trick in the book to keep Earls off the court. If she lost and the legislature's amendment passed, Republicans could create a new conservative majority on the high court. Then they could pass a new voter ID law and protect their gerrymandered election districts. The GOP would remain above accountability.

Senator McKissick warned what would happen if his Republican colleagues managed to reshape the judiciary. He said, "We've been able to historically look to the courts to provide open doors and to stand up for rights. But it's not so certain that that future will be as bright as it has been in the past. There's reason to believe that light will become far dimmer."

PART III

RESTORING CHECKS
AND BALANCES

CHAPTER 26

AN INDEPENDENT JUDICIARY

North Carolina voters protected democracy in 2018. They elected Earls to the state supreme court and rejected the legislature's court packing amendment. And with fairer districts in place, thanks to Earls' litigation, enough Democratic legislators were elected to end the GOP's veto-proof supermajority.

Earls was elected with around half the votes. The incumbent got just over one-third, and Anglin got the rest. In the end, Earls believed that the legislature's meddling in the race may have backfired. "It allowed me to run against the legislature, as much as Justice Jackson," she said.

When the election results were clear, the victorious candidate gave a speech with her supporters beside her. The crowd cheered and waved campaign signs with an image of Lady Justice, blindfolded and clad in a Tar Heel-blue robe. Her scales of justice were evenly balanced.

Justice-elect Earls reflected on the race. "We faced a huge uphill battle. Nothing was certain." She noted that litigation over the legislature's power grabs had kept them from knowing who was in the race and what the ballot would look like. But her supporters' hard work and commitment had won the race. Earls said, "We faced long odds together."

Her win was a clear victory for judicial independence. "We have misguided partisans in our state who believe that they should impeach justices who don't rule in their favor," Earls said, "By working together over the past year, we've shown that we can stand up for the importance of an independent judiciary … and stand up for the people's right to vote." She thanked her supporters for believing they could make a difference.

Earls promised that, after being sworn in as the court's 100th justice, she would "resist partisan attacks on the judicial branch, which must remain independent and impartial in order for our democracy to succeed and thrive." She called on the crowd to "move forward, without fear or favor" and continue the work of seeking equal justice. Earls quoted Nelson Mandela, "After climbing a great hill, one only finds that there are many more hills to climb."

As a lawyer, Earls and her organization had helped persuade courts to strike down the legislature's racially gerrymandered districts and a voter suppression law that targeted Black voters with "almost surgical precision." Now she would serve on a court with the power to strike down discriminatory state laws.

Her victory laid the groundwork for state courts to make elections fair again. In her first two years in office, the courts protected the rights of voters under the state constitution.

The courts issued crucial decisions that made the 2020 election much fairer. A judge in September 2020, for example, ruled that people with felony convictions can't be barred from voting solely because they still owe court fines or fees, citing the state constitution's ban on "property qualifications" for voting. Dennis Gaddy, a plaintiff in the case and an advocate for voting rights restoration, said "I'm ecstatic and just overjoyed."

The high court also finally acknowledged the persistent problem of racism in jury selection. The state supreme court had never before ruled for a defendant on the issue, despite statistical evidence of discrimination. In May 2020, Earls wrote the decision that broke prosecutors' winning streak at the high court.

A few weeks later, Earls wrote a decision that could help 130 of the 150 people on North Carolina's death row. The justices ruled that the legislature's repeal of the Racial Justice Act couldn't apply to those defendants who had already requested hearings on their racial discrimination claims.

In addition to electing Earls, the voters soundly rejected the amendments giving the legislature control over choosing judges and the state elections board. The judicial selection amendment was so unpopular that only seven of the state's 100 counties voted in favor of it. Two-thirds of voters rejected the idea of giving the legislature control over choosing judges.

Some Republicans and conservatives had opposed the amendment. The Koch brothers-backed Americans for Prosperity ran ads criticizing it, and the head of the North Carolina chapter referred to it as "partisan court packing." Along with the five former governors, the amendment was opposed by all six living former chief justices of the North Carolina Supreme Court.

Hunter, who was a Court of Appeals judge, said in an interview that he had helped legislators draft the amendment. He acknowledged that it faced "a lot of pushback" and conceded there were problems. But Hunter agreed with the goal of giving legislators some role in choosing judges, though he wouldn't support giving them total control, as in Virginia and South Carolina.

Progressives had rallied around a #NixAllSix opposition campaign, although four of the proposed amendments were approved. The effort included voting rights groups, Democrats, good government advocates, new groups like Indivisible, and many others.

In 2018, voters also elected enough Democratic legislators to end Republicans' power to override the governor's vetoes. The election districts had been redrawn, thanks to Earls' federal lawsuit, and the new ones didn't discriminate against Black voters. But the districts still seemed to favor Republicans. GOP candidates got less than half the votes in 2018, but they maintained a majority in both houses.

Once a new legislature was sworn in, Republicans would lose the unfettered legislative power they had enjoyed since 2013. The era of attacks on voting rights and judicial independence would soon be over. The end of the GOP supermajority meant an end to the GOP's quest to control state courts. If the amendment had been approved, there would have likely been another attempt to pack the state supreme court.

The voters secured the court's progressive majority. Earls' election meant that five out of seven justices were Democrats. In early 2019, Chief Justice Martin, one of only two Republicans on the court, took a position heading a law school in Virginia. Gov. Cooper appointed Beasley to lead the court.

Beasley was the first Black woman to head the state judiciary. Under her leadership, the court would make progress towards reforming some unfair aspects of the criminal justice system. And it would remove the giant portrait of former Chief Justice Ruffin, the brutal enslaver whose opinions sanctioned violence by other enslavers.

After Cooper appointed Beasley instead of Justice Newby, who had served on the court the longest, Republican legislators introduced a budget bill that slashed the budget of the new Chief Justice. But the cuts didn't last long. Lawmakers quickly restored funding for Beasley's office.

Before the supermajority left office in 2019, they held one last lame duck session. Though voters had rejected two of the legislature's amendments, they approved a constitutional voter ID mandate. They had also approved a constitutional right to hunt and fish, new rights for criminal victims, and a lowering of the state's cap on income taxes.

The voter ID amendment left it to the legislature to specify what type of ID is required, and though there was no deadline, lawmakers wanted to pass a new voter ID law before they lost the power to override the governor's veto.

CHAPTER 27

ONE FINAL ATTACK ON VOTING RIGHTS

In North Carolina, Republicans had a record of ginning up fear about voter fraud to justify voter suppression. They did it with their 2013 voter ID mandate, even though studies had shown that in-person voter fraud was extremely rare. They did to persuade citizens to pass the voter ID amendment in 2018. And they did it to justify the post-election voter ID law. Judges, however, have seen through the voter fraud lie.

When Gov. McCrory narrowly lost reelection in 2016, he blamed voter fraud. The outcome wasn't clear for weeks after Election Day. As Cooper amassed more votes, McCrory began making unfounded allegations of voter fraud. He accused dozens of people of voting while they were ineligible, because of felony convictions. Most of the accusations were unfounded, and several of the voters filed a libel lawsuit.

Two weeks after the election, a think tank funded by Pope filed a lawsuit in federal court, the Eastern District, against the board of elections. The lawsuit aimed to stop the board from certifying the results, claiming that thousands of votes shouldn't be counted until the voters' addresses were verified. The case was dismissed, and Cooper won by around 10,000 votes.

A couple of years after McCrory's unfounded voter fraud allegations, a Republican congressional candidate employed a political operative in Bladen County, near the Southeastern part of the state, who committed election fraud by manipulating mail-in ballots. The election was redone with a new Republican candidate, a state legislator who won the seat and maintained the 10-3 GOP control of the state's congressional seats.

Though no voters were accused of impersonating someone else, the stories about Bladen County fed the general perception that elections were vulnerable to voter fraud.

Before the GOP lost its veto-proof supermajority in 2019, the legislature met for one final lame-duck session to pass a new voter ID law. The NAACP and other civil rights groups pleaded with the legislature not to repeat the sins of 2013. They demanded that legislators allow voters to use student IDs and other government-issued identification.

Republicans announced on November 23, 2018, the day after Thanksgiving, that citizens could comment on the voter ID law at a public hearing the following Monday. An editorial from WRAL said the election results had sent a message that the lame-duck legislature should heed: "North Carolinians simply want their public officials to do the right things. End the secrecy, the games, the petty partisan paybacks and the take-it-or-leave-it lawmaking."

Democrats promised to work with them on a bill next year, but Republicans pushed forward without them.

The governor vetoed the bill. On December 18, 2018, the racially gerrymandered Republican supermajority overrode Cooper's veto one last time. A voter ID law was once again on the books in North Carolina.

Tomas Lopez, executive director of Democracy North Carolina, said the bill would "unnecessarily burden eligible North Carolinians' access to the ballot," particularly voters of color and "those most marginalized in our politics."

The law was blocked by a federal court, which emphasized the connection to the 2013 voter ID law that was struck down by federal judges. In December 2020, three judges on the Fourth U.S. Circuit Court of Appeals, including two Trump appointees, overturned that decision. The court said, "A legislature's past acts do not condemn the acts of a later legislature, which we must presume acts in good faith."

Democracy NC, SCSJ and other voting rights groups also filed a lawsuit in state court claiming that the voter ID bill was unconstitutional. The lawsuit argued the bill violated the North Carolina constitution's ban on racial discrimination, the right to vote in free elections, the ban on property requirements for voting, and the right to free speech.

The voter ID amendment did not authorize legislators to violate other provisions of the state constitution. SCSJ's Allison Riggs argued that lawmakers had "failed miserably" at balancing the voter ID mandate with other provisions of the constitution.

"Any legislative scheme that requires voters to present ID when voting must have fail-safe measures to ensure that not one single eligible voter is disenfranchised. Our state constitution demands it. This legislation does not do that," Riggs argued.

She argued the judges should block any implementation of the law, until they could decide if it's constitutional. Riggs asked the court, a panel of three judges, to act quickly.

The trial moved forward, and the legislature passed a law that delayed implementation of the voter ID bill until 2020. But the court didn't block the law. SCSJ asked the Court of Appeals to review the ruling.

In February 2020, days after voting began for the 2020 primary election, the North Carolina Court of Appeals blocked the voter ID requirement. The judges agreed that the new voter ID requirement would likely have a disproportionate impact on Black voters.

The court noted that the voter ID amendment "allows for exceptions to any voter-ID law, yet ... the General Assembly specifically left out types of IDs that African Americans disproportionately lack."

Naturally, Republicans were furious. Two legislators said in a joint statement, "Three elitist Democratic judges just decided that the people cannot amend their own Constitution, even though the voter ID amendment received more votes than any of the judges." They warned the judges that they would "have to answer for overturning the clear will of the voters come November."

CHAPTER 28

NOT FIT TO JUDGE

Trump managed a record number of judicial confirmations, including two conservative justices that shifted the High Court further to the right. These judges ruled against voting rights in the run-up to the 2020 election. Earls said Trump "made good on his promises for the courts." But one of his nominees, Thomas Farr, met relentless opposition from activists in North Carolina and around the country.

In the summer of 2018, some of these activists convened in Iowa, where they hoped to meet with the staff of Republican Sen. Chuck Grassley, head of the judiciary committee. But they had to settle for a group phone call with Michael Davis, a lawyer for the committee in D.C. They wore blue t-shirts calling Grassley a rubber-stamp for Trump's judges.

The activists spent their time on the call expressing concerns about horrible Trump nominees and the appalling lack of diversity. At the time, more than 90 percent of Trump's nominees were white. One of them pleaded with the Davis to take a closer look at Farr's relationship to Tom Ellis, his former law partner, mentor, and an unabashed white supremacist.

Davis responded, "To say that someone is a white supremacist is a serious allegation and it sounds to me like you don't want to have a serious conversation." When the activist mentioned Ellis' leading role in the Pioneer Fund, which funded junk science about the genetic superiority of white people, Davis seemed surprised. He claimed that this was the first he had heard of this, even though activists had raised the issue with Sen. Grassley and others on the Judiciary Committee for the past year.

Davis didn't back down on Grassley's support for Farr. When some activists pressed him on why so many Trump nominees refused to state that *Brown v. Board of Education* was correctly decided, Davis accused them of "gutter politics." The activists were seething with anger after the call.

The NAACP and Demand Justice, a progressive group founded to oppose Trump nominees, organized a rally to oppose Farr outside the U.S. Capitol in June 2018. Busloads of activists from North Carolina protested the nomination.

Barber called the GOP effort to seat Farr "an attempt to stack the courts with a lawyer who has a known history of supporting systemic racism, voter suppression, and anti-worker laws and unconstitutional legal theory." Barber said, "To support Farr is to support racism, disparate treatment, and anti-worker policies ... in the 21st century." He called out North Carolina Senators Tillis and Richard Burr for blocking the two Black women nominated to judgeships in the Eastern District by President Obama.

The NAACP said in a statement that Farr "learned how to intimidate Black voters from segregationist Sen. Jesse Helms and helped turn North Carolina into ground zero for voter suppression tactics."

Farr wasn't worthy to sit in judgment of anyone. But Republicans scheduled a vote in the Senate to move him forward. A few weeks after the 2018 election, Vice President Mike Pence cast a vote to break a tie vote and set Farr up for final confirmation.

The final vote was scheduled just a couple of months after the confirmation of Justice Kavanaugh. For many activists, emotions were still raw.

South Carolina Senator Tim Scott, the only Black Republican in Congress, had voted with his GOP colleagues to set Farr up for a final vote. Barber described Scott's vote to advance Farr as "what internalized racism and political delusion look like." Democrats inundated Scott with pleas to vote against Farr. Just six months earlier, the senator had sank a judicial nomination over concerns about the nominee's racist writings.

The next day, Scott announced that he wouldn't vote to confirm Farr. He said, "there are a lot of folks that can be judges" in North Carolina besides Farr. Scott cited a breaking story in the *Washington Post* about a decades-old DOJ memo that described Farr's role in Helms' voter intimidation campaign.

Trump withdrew Farr from consideration. Despite four nominations by two different presidents, Jesse Helms' former attorney would never become a judge. Barber credited Scott for doing the right thing.

Farr went back to his old job, defending Republicans from charges of racial discrimination.

CHAPTER 29

REPEALING TWO POWER GRABS

The legislature repealed two of its changes to the judiciary in 2019, under the threat of litigation in state court. Gov. Cooper filed one of the lawsuits, challenging the "court unpacking" bill. (*See chapter 16.*) Judge Bob Hunter's mandatory retirement date was approaching in the spring of 2019, and the bill would eliminate his seat after that happened. That would prevent Cooper from replacing Hunter and two other Republican judges on the Court of Appeals.

Though the judge ruled for the legislature, Republicans worried the state supreme court would overturn that decision. To head off that outcome, they repealed the bill. Hunter retired, and Cooper appointed his replacement.

A few months later, Hunter found himself back on the other side of the bench as an attorney. He filed a new racial gerrymandering lawsuit. The plaintiffs were Black voters in Charlotte and the Black judges who had been placed in overwhelmingly white election districts in the 2018 judicial redistricting bill.

(*See chapter 17.*) Kimberly Best was one of the judges, and she said many lawyers had turned them away before they found Hunter.

"I wasn't able to find anyone willing to take on the case," she said. Some lawyers looked at it through the lens of federal law, but the plaintiffs knew the state constitutional claims were more likely to succeed. They wanted to file the suit in state court.

One of Best's co-plaintiffs, Judge Donald Cureton, knew Hunter and set up a meeting. Best said he was a "divinely inspired" choice to represent them. "Judge Hunter's knowledge of election law was what did it," she said. And it didn't hurt that he was a Republican.

Hunter and his clients argued that the legislature had intentionally minimized the voting strength of communities of color, violating the bans on racial discrimination in the state and federal constitutions, as well as the VRA. Their complaint argued the new districts were "deliberately segregated along … racial lines" to give white voters more political power.

The plaintiffs argued that dividing counties into judicial districts violated state law and a constitutional requirement that laws establishing local courts must be "uniformly applicable." The state constitution also requires judges to reside in their districts, which were defined in state law as consisting "exclusively of one or more entire counties." Yet the new law required Charlotte judges to live in a specific subdistrict.

The defendants denied that they targeted Black voters. A former Republican legislative leader, U.S. Rep. Dan Bishop, filed an affidavit describing the process of drawing the districts. "I specified that no racial data be used," he swore. But newly discovered evidence had shown that the map-drawer had data on the racial breakdown of the new districts.

State legislators were once again defended by Farr. On November 18, 2019, the lawyers arrived at a courthouse in Raleigh, but there was confusion about which court would hear the case.

Farr walked in and, still unsure about the location, sat down on the hard wooden benches reserved for spectators. Hunter and his clients eventually filed in, and the parties took their places.

During their arguments, Farr seemed like he was caught off guard, as if it hadn't occurred to his clients that these districts might be racially gerrymandered. He denied that legislators had intentionally drawn a district that was 82 percent Black.

Hunter asked Judge Craig Croom to order a return to county-wide elections for District Court. He asked the court to act quickly, in time for the 2020 primaries. Hunter called the districts "horribly segregated" and said legislators had offered no justification for packing Black voters.

Farr argued that the case should be heard by a three-judge panel, and Croom seemed inclined to agree. He carefully read through Farr's motion, then called a late lunch break. He reconvened four minutes early and declined to dismiss the lawsuit.

Croom said the state supreme court would appoint a three-judge panel, and the justices understood that "time is of the essence." Filing for the 2020 elections would begin in early December.

After the hearing, legislators agreed to scrap the districts and quietly settled the lawsuit. The settlement agreement said the county would return to countywide elections in 2018. Some of the judges who had filed the lawsuit signed up to run. Judges Best and Cureton were reelected. And the legislature passed a bill in 2020 that undid the Charlotte districts for good.

CHAPTER 30

USURPING THE PEOPLE'S AUTHORITY

The North Carolina Supreme Court will hear a case in 2021 challenging the voter ID amendment itself. The lawsuit, filed in 2018 by the state NAACP and an environmental group, argued that the racially gerrymandered legislature had no authority to put the amendment on the ballot in 2018. The amendment had only passed by a few votes, which wouldn't have been possible without the illegal gerrymander.

The NAACP's lawsuit cited cases from the Reconstruction era, when state courts had settled election disputes between newly enfranchised Black voters and the white political establishment. The state supreme court had sided with the white establishment and declared Black officials "usurpers."

In 1890, for example, a disputed election was held in New Hanover County, a majority-Black county where elected Black leaders would soon be violently ousted by white supremacists in the only successful coup d'état in U.S. history. C.H. Thomas, a Black county resident, had complained that a small group of white "political overseers" controlled local elections.

After the election, a precinct registrar claimed that Thomas, who was his clerk, took the voter registration books and ran the 1890 election. Local officials then refused to certify the votes, which were crucial to the outcome of a judicial race. The head election official was Judge D.L. Russell, whom Thomas had claimed described Blacks as "savages" who were not "fit to govern."

The North Carolina Supreme Court sided with the white election officials. The opinion, written by a chief justice who had served in the Confederate Army, declared Thomas a usurper with no legal authority to conduct the election. The court overturned the election result.

More than a century later, the NAACP's new lawsuit offered the courts a chance to hold a group of all-white elected officials accountable for manipulating election districts in Black communities. The lawsuit could impose some accountability for the GOP supermajority that ruled the state for years.

In meetings with their allies, the NAACP had long insisted that they should stop lobbying the legislature, because it hadn't been legitimately elected. At their rallies, Reverends Barber and Spearman often referred to the legislature as illegitimate usurpers.

In March 2019, Judge Bryan Collins agreed with the NAACP and threw out the amendment. He said it was approved by a legislature "that did not represent the people of North Carolina." The court said the legislature "lost its claim to popular sovereignty" after federal courts ruled that it was the product of racially discriminatory election districts.

"The unconstitutional racial gerrymander tainted the 3/5 majority required by the state constitution, ... breaking the appropriate chain of popular sovereignty between North Carolina citizens and their representatives," Collins wrote.

In September 2020, two judges on the Court of Appeals overturned Judge Collins' decision. Republican Judge Chris Dillon wrote the ruling, which said that North Carolina's courts had never before asserted "the power to deprive the General Assembly of authority ... granted that body by our state constitution," and that includes the power to put constitutional amendments on the ballot.

Dillon discussed the history of the federal lawsuit challenging the racially gerrymandered districts. He claimed that when the legislature drew new election districts in 2011, it had "sought to engage in partisan gerrymandering," even though the U.S. Supreme Court affirmed that the districts were racially gerrymandered.

The majority's decision seemed to accept Republicans' excuse for shoehorning Black voters into districts where they were a majority. Dilllon said that lawmakers' goal "was to ensure that their maps would not run afoul" of the VRA, but he also acknowledged that federal courts had rejected their VRA justification.

A concurring opinion by a Republican judge attacked Collins' 2019 ruling and claimed it wasn't grounded in state law.

The dissent from Judge Reuben Young, a Black Democrat, laid out why he thought the legislature had lost some of its authority under the state constitution: "Only a legislature formed by the will of the people, representing our population in truth and fact, may ... amend or alter the central document of this state's laws." Young warned that "if an unlawfully-formed legislature could indeed amend the constitution, it could do so to grant itself the veneer of legitimacy."

In a footnote, Young noted that the 2018 voter ID amendment was "designed to prevent citizens from unlawfully voting in our elections. And yet, this amendment was proposed by a General Assembly which was, itself, unlawfully formed."

The majority's decision repeatedly claimed that the federal courts "did not believe" that the legislature had lost its authority to govern, but it didn't mention that the federal judges had explicitly said it was "an unsettled question of state law" that they couldn't resolve.

Dillon's decision declared emphatically that "**partisan gerrymandering is legal**" under the U.S. Supreme Court's rulings. But he didn't even mention that state courts had ruled, a year earlier, that partisan gerrymandering violates the North Carolina Constitution.

CHAPTER 31

BREAKING THEIR GRIP ON POWER

By 2019, Trump had reshaped the U.S. Supreme Court by appointing Justices Kavanaugh and Gorsuch. In June 2019, the Court threw out the partisan gerrymandering lawsuit challenging North Carolina's Congressional districts. (*See chapter 20.*) The opinion by Chief Justice Roberts said, "To hold that legislators cannot take partisan interests into account when drawing district lines would essentially countermand the Framers' decision to entrust districting to political entities."

Rep. Lewis had stated their intention to skew the districts in favor of Republicans, and the U.S. Supreme Court wasn't going to do anything to stop them. The justices overturned a lower court's ruling to strike down the districts. But the opinion, written by Roberts, noted that "state constitutions can provide standards and guidance for state courts to apply."

North Carolina courts promptly accepted his invitation. First, a lawsuit by Common Cause led to detailed statistical evidence that proved it was almost impossible for voters to choose a

Democratic state legislature.

The court admitted evidence from the "Hofeller files," the documents recovered from the hard drives of the deceased gerrymandering guru Thomas Hofeller. The files were discovered by Hofeller's estranged daughter. And a state court had rejected Republicans' attempt to keep them sealed.

Statistician Jowei Chen explained how some of the files showed that Hofeller had sorted voters along racial and partisan lines, crafting election districts that would keep Republicans in power.

Lawmakers had been prohibited by a federal court from using racial data to draw the maps, but Hofeller's files included racial data. Republicans had told the federal court that race wasn't used to draw the districts.

Farr defended the legislature and questioned the relevancy of the Hofeller files, which he called a "sideshow." The GOP claimed that the "plaintiffs were attempting to create a bogeyman out of a dead map drawer to distract from the weakness of [their] case."

The court ordered lawmakers to quickly draw new districts. A unanimous, bipartisan panel of three judges ruled that partisan gerrymandering violates the rights of voters under the state constitution. The court said that "elections are not free when partisan actors have tainted future elections by specifically and systematically designing the contours of the election districts for partisan purposes." The judges found that "the carefully crafted maps" had determined which party controlled the legislature.

The court also ruled that extreme gerrymandering violates the rights to freedom of speech and assembly, as well as equal protection, under the state constitution. The judges noted that the North Carolina Supreme Court has interpreted these rights more broadly than their counterparts in the U.S. Constitution.

The ruling came down in September 2019, a few months before candidates began filing to run in the 2020 primary election. Lawmakers were ordered to promptly go back to the drawing board. They had to fix the districts that had kept them in power, even though they got fewer total votes in the last election.

A new lawsuit was quickly filed against the congressional districts, and the state supreme court assigned the same three-judge panel to hear the case. The plaintiffs wanted the court to act quickly. They argued the case was "straightforward," citing Lewis' stated goal of districts that elected Republicans to 10 out of 13 districts. (At a summit on gerrymandering, Farr had recently claimed that Lewis was "just joking" when he listed the partisan criteria for drawing the districts.)

The plaintiffs wanted swift action. "North Carolinians have voted in unconstitutional congressional districts in every election this decade... They should not be forced to do so again." Republicans argued there wasn't enough time to redraw the districts before candidate filing began.

The judges weren't buying their delay tactics. The Hofeller files had revealed that the maps could be redrawn faster than legislators had claimed during the racial gerrymandering litigation.

The court ordered new districts within a week-and-a-half. The 357-page order laid out how legislators violated the state constitution by drawing election districts "with a predominant intent to favor voters aligned with one political party at the expense of other voters."

Former U.S. Attorney General Eric Holder, whose organization backed the suit, praised the ruling. Holder said, "Now—finally—the era of Republican gerrymandering in the state is coming to an end."

Republicans again accused the courts of exceeding their authority. Senate leader Phil Berger's response made clear the connection between judicial elections and the court's rulings. "With judges deciding behind closed doors how many members of Congress from each party is acceptable, judicial elections have become the most consequential in America," he said.

Despite their disappointment, Republicans agreed to redraw

the lines again. On September 9, Sen. Paul Newton kicked off the process by claiming that "no one thought partisan gerrymandering was wrong or evil" before the court ruling. Barber and many others had both railed against gerrymandering and challenged it in court.

Newton claimed that voters expected their elected representatives to "leverage" redistricting for partisan advantage, but he conceded, "the rules of the road have now changed" with the state court ruling.

For the first time, the redistricting process was live-streamed on YouTube. Sen. Blue called it the "most transparent redistricting process in history." The feed showed lawmakers changing lines they didn't like.

Citizens watched live as legislators used a lottery ball machine to select a map. They had numbered balls that represented one of five potential maps that had been drawn by Chen, the expert witness.

Of the 1,000 maps drawn by Chen's software, legislators chose from among the five most compact. Some observers pointed out that the problem the court ordered legislators to solve wasn't a lack of compactness. The real problem was the unfair partisan skewing of the districts. And the court had merely ordered legislators to "make reasonable efforts" to improve the districts' compactness.

Sam Wang, who runs the Princeton Gerrymandering Project, said in an interview with Facing South that more compact maps "tend to favor Republicans." Wang said, "To make an analogy to card games, a stacked deck can't produce a fair deal.... And I have some questions about the deck."

Wang noted that Chen's 1,000 maps were also scored on whether they were slanted towards one party or the other. He suggested lawmakers should start with the maps that didn't favor one party or another. But they pressed forward and chose from among the most compact maps.

The districts were passed along party lines and were accepted by the courts. Experts said they are still slanted towards the GOP, but not as much as the old districts.

Lawmakers then moved on to the biased congressional districts. North Carolina voters had cast more votes for Democrats in 2018, but 10 of the state's 13 seats remained under Republican control.

Election law experts had questioned whether the court would have enough time to hold a trial and draw new districts, but the legal questions were the same as in the first trial. And since law-makers had announced their intention to draw a map that elected 10 Republicans, the judges didn't have trouble reaching a decision and ordered new districts within days.

Legislators tried to have the lawsuit over congressional districts moved to federal court, even though the case was about the state constitution. They even argued that redrawing the districts would violate the federal court's ruling in the racial gerrymandering case. Their appeal was rejected by a panel of three judges on the 4th Circuit, including Judges Motz and Gregory.

The election districts were redrawn, as the state court ordered, and experts pointed out that the new districts would make elections more competitive. Several Republican members of Congress didn't seek reelection in 2020. The less-skewed North Carolina districts were pivotal to Democrats maintaining their control of Congress in the 2020 election.

The rulings were a vindication for voters and activists like Barber, who had been calling for a return to the foundational principles of the North Carolina Constitution. Since the beginning of Moral Mondays, Barber had noted that the Constitution requires that the government's power be exercised "for the good of the whole."

CONCLUSION

"WE CHOSE NOT TO STAND DOWN"

These court rulings were a clear victory for democracy. They empowered North Carolina voters, who lived under an unaccountable, power-hungry regime for a decade. None of it would have been possible if the legislature had succeeded in its attempted court takeovers.

Republicans had tried everything to keep state courts from undoing their power grabs. They invented new ways to manipulate elections and pack the courts. In 2016, Republicans floated a scheme to pack the state supreme court, by creating two new seats for the lame-duck Republican governor to fill. They backed down amid a national outcry, but they spent the next two years trying everything they could to get their judges on the bench.

Then in 2018, they put a constitutional amendment on the ballot that would have opened the door to another lame-duck court packing scheme. But the voters said no.

If the GOP's plots had succeeded, the state supreme court wouldn't have required the legislature to draw new election districts. And the Republican-led legislature would still be above accountability. But these power grabs failed. North Carolina voters protected judicial independence, and the courts protected democracy.

As head of the nationwide Poor People's Campaign, Barber took the "Moral Monday" model to other state capitols. "We believe North Carolina is the crucible," he said. "If you're going to change the country, you've got to change the South. If you're going to change the South, you've got to focus on these state capitols."

The reverend has called for a third Reconstruction of American society. He travels the country telling the story of the fight in North Carolina. "Everywhere we've gone, from deep in the heart of Dixie to Wisconsin.... I heard a longing for a moral movement that plows deep into our souls and recognizes that the attacks we face today are not a sign of our weakness, but rather the manifestation of a worrisome fear among the governing elites that their days are numbered and the hour is late."

Barber declared victory in fighting the North Carolina legislature's worst voter suppression measures. "We chose not to stand down," he told Charlotte's NPR station in August 2020. "There were people who told us to accept photo ID, and we said no. And it was a four-year battle, but we won."

Earls continues to fight for fairness as a high court justice. She hopes to "make more explicit the ways in which the decisions of our court are systematically disadvantaging people... primarily based on race and income," she said. In the summer of 2020, as Black Lives Matter protests erupted in Raleigh, Earls and Chief Justice Beasley both talked frankly about systemic racism and the implicit biases that influence everyone, including judges.

In the 2020 election, voters ousted Beasley and another Democrat, leaving a 4-3 Democratic majority. Justice Newby had challenged Beasley, after Cooper declined to appoint him to the leadership spot, and he was elected to lead the court by just a few hundred votes. The GOP has the chance to win a majority on the court in 2022.

The Republican legislature will redraw districts in 2021 with new Census data, and they could try to gerrymander elections again.

This time, however, they will draw election districts under the guidelines established by state courts in 2019. The courts can step in early to stop unfair partisan gerrymandering. There's a chance that, in the next decade, North Carolinians will be governed by a legislature that actually responds to what voters want.

Over the past decade, during endless litigation, support has only grown for a nonpartisan redistricting system. And many Republicans agree on the need to change the status quo.

Progressives are hopeful that a future legislature will reverse the GOP's changes to election laws, expand Medicaid, and restore funding for public schools. Kromm and voting rights groups are pushing a broad, good-government platform that protects voting rights and includes a new judicial public financing program to keep candidates from relying on wealthy campaign donors.

The GOP legislature that has ruled the state for the past decade will leave behind a legacy of racial discrimination and attacking the foundations of democracy. Republicans repeatedly violated the constitutional system of checks and balances. And when courts struck down their power grabs, they tried to pack the high court and rewrite the constitution's separation of powers clause. But the courts and the voters stood in their way.

The North Carolina constitution says, "All political power is vested in and derived from the people." The voters and the courts made that true.

EPILOGUE

A PAGE FROM THE NORTH CAROLINA PLAYBOOK

With the 2020 Census concluded, state legislatures are preparing to redraw election districts next year. This means that control of state supreme courts is even more important. In states without nonpartisan redistricting, the courts are likely to be the only check on extreme gerrymandering.

Republican lawmakers understand this, and the power grabs employed in North Carolina have spread to other states. Kromm warned in 2018 that North Carolina was a "test case." GOP legislatures have begun targeting the other branches of government when voters choose Democrats. As Nichol wrote in *Indecent Assembly*, "North Carolina legislators taught them that perhaps you are not required to actually turn over the keys to the governor's mansion. It is not necessary to respect the results of an intervening election."

When midwestern voters elected Democratic governors in 2018, lame-duck legislatures transferred power from the executive to the legislative branch. As in North Carolina, Wisconsin lawmakers tied the hands of the governor and attorney general, when it comes to lawsuits against the state. The conservative Wisconsin Supreme Court upheld nearly all of the laws passed by the 2018 lame-duck legislature.

Lawmakers have lashed at courts when they don't like their rulings. Republican legislators in Pennsylvania introduced articles of impeachment for justices who struck down gerrymandered election maps in 2018. The court ruled that partisan gerrymandering violated the state constitutional right to "free and equal" elections.

The Pennsylvania legislature also passed a constitutional amendment that would end statewide high court elections and create election districts, which lawmakers would be in charge of drawing. This would open the door to the same kind of judicial gerrymandering that happened to voters in Charlotte, North Carolina.

Republicans at the state and federal level have broken norms around judicial selection to get their judges in power. These leaders see that demographic trends spell trouble for their party, whose leaders don't seem to be willing to build bridges to reach non-white voters. Instead, they want to keep suppressing votes. Their power grabs are often unconstitutional, but that won't matter if they succeed in taking control of the courts.

President Trump and the U.S. Senate succeeded in their efforts to transform the federal courts, confirming more than 200 of the president's nominees. Many of these judges have a history of defending voter suppression, and voting rights advocates are increasingly looking to state courts for justice.

Republican governors in several states have sought more control over judicial nominating commissions, which are supposed to ensure that the most qualified judges reach the bench. Montana Republicans eliminated their state's commission in 2021.

When courts in Kansas and Oklahoma struck down laws limiting access to abortion, lawmakers responded with bills to give them more control over choosing justices. Arizona Gov. Doug Ducey has stacked his state's judicial nominating commission with Republicans, even though the constitution establishes a bipartisan system. The commission will play a key role in the state's upcoming redistricting, appointing a fifth, tie-breaking member of a bipartisan redistricting commission.

As in North Carolina, some Republicans have explored the idea of ending judicial elections altogether. Voters in Houston elected a historically diverse slate of Democratic judicial candidates in 2018, and this led Texas lawmakers to begin exploring the idea of ending or limiting judicial elections. A constitutional amendment introduced in February 2019 would have moved to an appointment system, but only in big cities like Houston.

The RSLC has moved beyond North Carolina to spend millions dominating high court elections in other states. The group, which receives funding from the dark money Judicial Crisis Network, has run ads attacking judges in nonpartisan high court races.

In the first six months of 2020, the RSLC reported $2.9 million in spending in nonpartisan races in Arkansas, West Virginia, and Wisconsin, according to the Brennan Center. The RSLC supported two incumbents in West Virginia with ads worth more than $500,000, far more than any other group or candidate. The justices were both appointed to replace justices who resigned in 2018, after the entire court was impeached over a fiscal scandal.

Politicians and corporate special interests are trying to get their preferred justices on state supreme courts. Given what's happened with federal courts, these justices are crucial to protecting individual rights and safeguarding democracy. State courts are the last chance to stop partisan gerrymandering and discriminatory, unfair voting laws.

Voters must stop legislators' power grabs if they want courts that protect their rights. The war for American democracy can't be won without the courts.

ENDNOTES

PROLOGUE
Rev. William Barber and Jonathan Wilson-Hartgrove, *The Third Reconstruction* (Boston: Beacon Press, 2016), 109.

INTRODUCTION
Jedidiah Purdy, "North Carolina's Partisan Crisis," *The New Yorker*, December 20, 2016, https://www.newyorker.com/news/news-desk/north-carolinas-partisan-crisis.

Rev. William Barber, "In North Carolina, the March Against Extreme Policies is Working," *Sojourners*, February 14, 2017, https://sojo.net/articles/faith-action/north-carolina-march -against-extreme-policies-working.

Mark Joseph Stern, "North Carolina Republicans' Legislative Coup is an Attack on Democracy," *Slate*, December 15, 2016, https://slate.com/human-interest/2016/12/north-carolina-legislative -coup-an-attack-on-democracy.html.

Ruth Ben-Ghiat, *Strongmen: Mussolini to the Present* (New York: W.W. Norton & Company, 2020), 5.

Andrew Reynolds, "North Carolina is No Longer Classified as a Democracy" *News & Observer*, December 22, 2016, http://www.newsobserver.com/opinion/op-ed/article122593759.html.

Sharon McCloskey, "Win the Courts, Win the War," *N.C. Policy Watch*, December 15, 2015, http:// www.ncpolicywatch.com/2015/12/15/win-the-courts-win-the-war/.

Tara Golshan, "North Carolina Wrote the Playbook in Michigan and Wisconsin," *Vox*, December 5, 2018, https://www.vox.com/policy-and-politics/2018/12/5/18125544/north-carolina -power-grab-wisconsin-michigan-lame-duck.

CHAPTER 1
Paul Rosenberg, "This is How the GOP Rigged Congress," *Salon*, June 13, 2016, https://www. salon.com/2016/06/13/this_is_how_the_gop_rigged_congress_the_secret_plan_that_ handcuffed_obamas_presidency_but_backfired_in_donald_trump/.

David Daley, *Ratf**ked: The True Story Behind the Secret Plan to Steal American Democracy* (New York: W.W. Norton & Company, 2016), 5-17.

"Republican State Leadership Cmte: Top Contributors 2010," OpenSecrets.org, last accessed on February 16, 2021, https://www.opensecrets.org/527s/527cmtedetail_contribs.php?ein=050532524&cycle=2010.

Jane Mayer, "State for Sale," *The New Yorker*, October 3, 2011, https://www.newyorker.com/magazine/2011/10/10/state-for-sale.

Chris Kromm, "Power and Justice: Duke Energy Extends Influence to N.C. Courts," *Facing South*, March 7, 2014, https://www.facingsouth.org/2014/03/power-and-justice-duke-energy-extends-influence-to.html.

Sue Sturgis, "Why is GOP Mega-Donor Art Pope Distancing Himself from Controversial Big-Money Groups?" *Facing South*, October 9, 2013, https://www.facingsouth.org/2013/10/why-is-gop-mega-donor-art-pope-distancing-himself-.html.

Chris Kromm, "Art Pope's Big Day: Republican Benefactor Fueled GOP Capture of NC Legislature," *Facing South*, November 9, 2010, https://www.facingsouth.org/2010/11/art-popes-big-day-republican-benefactor-fueled-gop.html.

"John Adams Hyman," A North Carolina History Online Resource, last accessed on February 16, 2021, https://www.ncpedia.org/anchor/john-adams-hyman.

Will Doran, "Long-serving Durham Legislator Paul Luebke Dies at 70," *News & Observer*, October 30, 2016, http://www.newsobserver.com/news/politics-government/state-politics/article111489907.html.

Gary Robertson, "Cooper Sues to Alter Powerful NC Government Rules Panel," *Associated Press*, August 28, 2020, https://apnews.com/article/00cdcf8f5e7ab919d4aaed10b117f082.

Ella Nilson, "North Carolina's Extreme Gerrymandering Could Save the House Republican Majority," *Vox*, May 18, 2018, https://www.vox.com/policy-and-politics/2018/5/8/17271766/north-carolina-gerrymandering-2018-midterms-partisan-redistricting.

John Hood, "It's a Republican Gerrymander," *Carolina Journal*, July 14, 2011, https://www.carolinajournal.com/opinion-article/its-a-republican-gerrymander/.

Jaeah Lee, Zaineb Mohammed, and Adam Serwer, "Now That's What I Call Gerrymandering!" *Mother Jones*, November 14, 2012, https://www.motherjones.com/politics/2012/11/republicans-gerrymandering-house-representatives-election-chart/.

Eric McGhee and Nicholas Stephanopoulos, 2015, "Partisan Gerrymandering and the Efficiency Gap," *University of Chicago Law Review* 82, no. 2, https://chicagounbound.uchicago.edu/uclrev/vol82/iss2/4.

Ari Berman, "The Courts Won't End Gerrymandering. Eric Holder Has a Plan to Fix it Without Them," *Mother Jones*, July 2019, https://www.motherjones.com/politics/2019/07/the-courts-wont-end-gerrymandering-eric-holder-has-a-plan-to-fix-it-without-them/.

Rev. William Barber, "Racist Gerrymandering Created a GOP Stronghold in the South. We Must Fight Back," *Democracy Now*, June 10, 2019, https://www.democracynow.org/2019/6/10/rev_william_barber_racist_gerrymandering_created.

"Supreme Court Rejects Appeal Over NC Voter ID Law," *WRAL*, updated July 13, 2018, https://www.wral.com/supreme-court-reject-appeal-over-nc-voter-id-law/16702517/.

Richard Fausset, "2 New Limits on Voting in North Carolina are Rejected by U.S. Court," *New York Times*, October 2, 2014, https://www.nytimes.com/2014/10/02/us/2-new-limits-on-voting-in-north-carolina-are-rejected-by-us-court.html.

CHAPTER 2

Melissa Boughton, "Anita Earls Sworn in as New Supreme Court Justice in Standing Room Only Ceremony," *NC Policy Watch*, January 4, 2019, http://pulse.ncpolicywatch.org/2019/01/04/anita-earls-sworn-in-as-new-supreme-court-justice-in-standing-room-only-ceremony/.

Ari Berman, *Give Us the Ballot* (New York: Farrar, Straus, and Giroux, 2015), 173.

Anita Earls, "Could This Put an End to Gerrymandering?," *The Nation*, June 26, 2017, https://www.thenation.com/article/archive/could-this-put-an-end-to-gerrymandering/.

Ari Berman, "How the GOP is Resegregating the South," *The Nation*, January 31, 2012, https://www.thenation.com/article/archive/how-gop-resegregating-south/.

Nicole Campbell and Frank Stasio, "Exploring the Life, Legacy, and Unfinished Work of Julius Chambers," *WUNC*, August 15, 2013, https://www.wunc.org/post/exploring-life-legacy-and-unfinished-work-julius-l-chambers.

CHAPTER 3

Berman, *Give Us the Ballot*, 187-191.

Tinsley Yarbrough, *Race and Redistricting: The Shaw-Cromartie Cases* (Lawrence, Kansas: The University Press of Kansas, 2002), 15-16, 52, 92.

Robert N. Hunter, Jr., (1987) "Racial Gerrymandering and the Voting Rights Act in North Carolina," *Campbell Law Review* 9, no.2, https://scholarship.law.campbell.edu/clr/vol9/iss2/2/.

"Helms' Campaign Denies it Tried to Intimidate Black Voters," *Associated Press*, February 27, 1992, https://apnews.com/article/52589f9f339ea20d62e3c217fdecae1e.

Jeffrey Billman, "For Decades, Thomas Farr Helped N.C. Republicans Suppress Black Voters," *Indy Week*, November 28, 2018.

Pope v. Blue, 809 F. Supp. 392 (W.D.N.C. 1992).

Theodore Johnson, "How Conservatives Turned the 'Color-Blind' Constitution Against Racial Progress," *The Atlantic*, November 19, 2019, https://www.theatlantic.com/ideas/archive/2019/11/colorblind-constitution/602221/.

Yarbrough, *Race and Redistricting*, 69, 118, 164.

Shaw v. Reno, 509 U.S. 630 (1993).

Easley v. Cromartie, 532 U.S. 234 (2001).

Anita Earls, Leeanne Quatrucci, and Emily Wynes, (2007-2008) "Voting Rights in North Carolina: 1982-2006," *California Review of Law and Social Justice* 17, https://gould.usc.edu/students/journals/rlsj/issues/assets/docs/issue_17/05_North_Carolina_Macro.pdf.

Stephenson v. Bartlett, 562 S.E.2d 377 (N.C. 2002).

Seth Whitaker, "State Redistricting Law: Stephenson v. Bartlett and the Judicial Promotion of Electoral Competition," *Virginia Law Review* 91, https://www.jstor.org/stable/3649423?refreqid=excelsior%3A832ae6c7625202a2bcdea00a948477a0&seq=1.

Ballotpedia, "North Carolina 1970 Ballot Measures," https://ballotpedia.org/North_Carolina_1970_ballot_measures.

CHAPTER 4

Tyler Dukes and Heather Leah, "Historical Background of Confederate Monuments Removed from State Capitol Grounds," *WRAL*, Updated July 2, 2020, https://www.wral.com/take-a-tour-of-the-capitol-s-confederate-monuments/16904598/.

Billy Corriher, "NC Courts Grapple with Monuments to Jurist who Brutalized the Enslaved," *Facing South*, June 30, 2020, https://www.facingsouth.org/2020/06/nc-courts-grapple-monuments-jurist-who-brutalized-enslaved.

Billy Corriher, "Louisiana and North Carolina High Courts Remove Confederate Iconography," *Facing South*, January 14, 2021, https://www.facingsouth.org/2021/01/louisiana-and-north-carolina-high-courts-remove-confederate-iconography.

State v. Mann, 13 N.C. 263 (1829).

State v. Caesar, 31 N.C. 391 (1849).

Mark Davis, *A Warren Court of Our Own: The Exum Court and the Expansion of Individual Rights in North Carolina* (Durham, North Carolina: Carolina Academic Press, 2020), 25-44, 153-156.

Argument, *Dickson v. Rucho*, North Carolina Supreme Court, January 10, 2012, available at https://www.ncappellatecourts.org/videos/sc/2012/201PA12-2.wmv.

Alabama Legislative Caucus v. Alabama, 135 S.Ct. 1257 (2015).

Dickson v. Rucho, 367 N.C. 542 (2014).

Dickson v. Rucho, 135 S.Ct. 1843 (2015).

Dickson v. Rucho, 781 S.E.2d 404 (N.C. 2015).

Jurisdictional Statement, *North Carolina v. Covington*, November 14, 2016, https://www.scotusblog.com/wp-content/uploads/2017/06/16-649-jursidictional-statement-1.pdf.

CHAPTER 5

Berman, "How the GOP is Resegregating the South."

Brentin Mock, "NAACP Appealing North Carolina Redistricting Ruling," *Facing South*, July 30, 2013, https://www.facingsouth.org/2013/07/naacp-appealing-north-carolina-redistricting-rulin.html.

Sharon McCloskey, "More Questions in the Redistricting Case," *NC Policy Watch*, May 8, 2013, http://www.ncpolicywatch.com/2013/05/08/more-questions-in-the-redistricting-case/.

Ken Raymond, "NAACP's Gamesmanship Rings Hollow on New Maps," *Winston-Salem Journal*, December 13, 2012, https://journalnow.com/opinion/columnists/naacps-gamesmanship-rings-hollow-on-new-maps/article_6bfb430d-0c9f-595b-a3ed-d933a8725d25.html.

Anita Earls, "Could This Put an End to Gerrymandering?," *The Nation*, June 26, 2017, https://www.thenation.com/article/archive/could-this-put-an-end-to-gerrymandering/.

CHAPTER 6

U.S. Senate, Committee on the Judiciary, Bills to Amend the Voting Rights Act of 1965, 97th Congress, 2nd sess., 1982, 413-416, https://books.google.com/books?id=WH4tKTHftfsC&printsec=frontcover#v=onepage&q&f=false.

Shelby County v. Holder, 133 S.Ct. 2612 (2013).

Berman, *Give Us the Ballot*, prologue, chap. 10.

WRAL, "NC Voter ID Bill Moving Ahead with Supreme Court Ruling," June 25, 2013, https://www.wral.com/nc-senator-voter-id-bill-moving-ahead-with-ruling/12591669/.

N.C. General Assembly, House, *Voter Information Verification Act*, HB 589, 2013 sess. https://www.ncleg.gov/Sessions/2013/Bills/House/PDF/H589v9.pdf.

William Wan, "Inside the Republican Creation of the North Carolina Voting Bill Dubbed the Monster Law," *Washington Post*, September 1, 2016, https://www.washingtonpost.com/politics/courts_law/inside-the-republican-creation-of-the-north-carolina-voting-bill-dubbed-the-monster-law/2016/09/01/79162398-6adf-11e6-8225-fbb8a6fc65bc_story.html.

Jim Rutenberg, "A Dream Undone," *The New York Times Magazine*, July 29, 2015, https://www.nytimes.com/2015/07/29/magazine/voting-rights-act-dream-undone.html.

Berman, *Give Us the Ballot*, chap. 10.

Ari Berman, "North Carolina Republicans Escalate Attack on Student Voting," *The Nation*, August 20, 2013, https://www.thenation.com/article/archive/north-carolina-republicans-escalate-attack-student-voting/.

Ari Berman, "North Carolina Passes the Country's Worst Voter Suppression Law," *The Nation*, July 30, 2013, https://billmoyers.com/2013/07/30/north-carolina-passes-the-countrys-worst-voter-suppression-law/.

Pat McCrory, "Why I Signed the Voter ID Law," *News & Observer*, August 12, 2013, https://www.newsobserver.com/2013/08/12/3102124/gov-pat-mccrory-why-i-signed-the.html.

German Lopez, "Longtime Republican Consultant: If Black People Voted Republican, Voter ID Laws Wouldn't Happen," *Vox*, September 2, 2016, https://www.vox.com/2016/9/2/12774066/voter-id-laws-racist.

Zachary Roth, "Black Residents in NC Fear Losing The Ability to Vote," *MSNBC*, August 13, 2013, https://www.msnbc.com/the-last-word/black-residents-north-carolina-fear-losing-msna76324.

Ari Berman, "Hundreds of Voters are Disenfranchised by North Carolina's New Voting Restrictions," *The Nation*, September 10, 2014, https://www.thenation.com/article/archive/hundreds-voters-are-disenfranchised-north-carolinas-new-voting-restrictions/.

Petition for Certiorari denied: *North Carolina v. North Carolina NAACP*, 831 F.3d 204 (4th Cir. 2016), March 2017, http://www.judicialwatch.org/wp-content/uploads/2017/03/North-Carolina-Voter-ID-Cert-Petition-FINAL-833.pdf.

Allen Smith, "94-year-old Rosanell Eaton is at the Center of Voting Rights Case," *Insider*, January 25, 2016, https://www.businessinsider.com/rosanell-eaton-voter-id-rights-north-carolina-2016-1.

"Democracy NC Celebrates Supreme Court's Decision on Monster Law," Democracy North Carolina, https://democracync.org/news/democracy-nc-celebrates-supreme-courts-decision-monster-law/.

North Carolina v. North Carolina NAACP, 831 F.3d 204 (4th Cir. 2016).

Washington Post, "Senate Confirms First Black Female Judge to 9th Circuit Court," July 22, 2000, https://www.washingtonpost.com/archive/politics/2000/07/22/senate-confirms-first-black-female-judge-to-9th-circuit-court/867e34b7-486b-4caf-87f2-e69d5c1ee66e/.

Oral Argument, *North Carolina Conference of the NAACP v. North Carolina*, 4th Cir., June 21, 2016, https://www.ca4.uscourts.gov/OAarchive/mp3/16-1468-20160621.mp3.

Mac McClelland, "Inside the Knock-Down, Drag-Out Fight to Turn North Carolina Blue," *Mother Jones*, November/December 2016, https://www.motherjones.com/politics/2016/10/north-carolina-voting-rights-hb2-naacp-lgbt-trans-pope/.

CHAPTER 7

U.S. Rep. Bobby Rush, "Honoring Judge Roger L. Gregory of the United States Court of Appeal for the Fourth Circuit," U.S. Congress. Congressional Record. 114th Cong., 2nd sess., 2016. Vol. 162, 1072-1073, https://www.govinfo.gov/content/pkg/CREC-2016-07-08/html/CREC-2016-07-08-pt1-PgE1072.htm.

Harris v. McCrory, 159 F.Supp.3d 600 (M.D.N.C. 2016).

WFAE, "12th, 1st Congressional Districts Must be Redrawn, Federal Court Rules," February 6, 2016, https://www.wfae.org/local-news/2016-02-06/12th-1st-congressional-districts-must-be-redrawn-federal-court-rules.

Dan Way, "Legislators Get an Earful at Redistricting Hearings," *Carolina Journal*, February 16, 2016, https://www.carolinajournal.com/news-article/legislators-get-an-earful-at-redistricting-hearings/.

Transcript of N.C. General Assembly, Joint Committee on Redistricting, February 16, 2016, available at Amended Complaint, *League of Women Voters v. Rucho*, 279 F.Supp.3d 587 (M.D.N.C. 2018), exhibit B, https://www.brennancenter.org/sites/default/files/legal-work/LWV_v_Rucho_AmendedComplaint.pdf.

David Daley, "To Fix Racial Gerrymandering, North Carolina Republicans Considered an All-White Slate," *The Intercept*, October 30, 2019, https://theintercept.com/2019/10/30/north-carolina-gerrymandering-maps-redistricting/.

Covington v. North Carolina, 283 F.Supp.3d 410 (M.D.N.C. 2018).

Covington v. North Carolina, 585 U.S. ___ (2018), https://www.brennancenter.org/sites/default/files/legal-work/2018-6-28-585-Summary%20Order.pdf.

Elie Mystal, "4 Libs and … Clarence Thomas Unite to Smack Down North Carolina's Racial Gerrymandering," *Above the Law*, May 25, 2017, https://abovethelaw.com/2017/05/4-libs-and-clarence-thomas-unite-to-smack-north-carolinas-racial-gerrymandering/.

Plaintiffs' Objections to Defendants' Remedial Districts and Memorandum of Law, *Covington v. North Carolina*, 283 F.Supp.3d 410 (M.D.N.C.), September 15, 2017, https://www.brennancenter.org/sites/default/files/legal-work/Covington_Plaintiffs ObjectionstoRemedialDistricts.pdf.

Legislative Defendants' Response to Plaintiffs' Objections, *Covington v. North Carolina*, 283 F.Supp.3d 410 (M.D.N.C.), September 22, 2017, https://www.brennancenter.org/sites/default/files/legal-work/Covington_Defendants-Response-to-Plaintiffs-Objections.pdf.

David Daley, *Unrigged: How Americans are Battling Back to Save Democracy* (New York: Liveright Publishing Corp., 2020), chap. 5-7.

CHAPTER 8

"HKonJ 2013: If We Believe," NC Forward Together Movement Channel, February 1, 2013, https://www.youtube.com/watch?v=-fAtEt9MtEo&t=8s.

Barber and Wilson-Hartgrove, *The Third Reconstruction*, 13, 54, 60-63, 98, 105, 108, 119, and 128.

Dr. Timothy Tyson, "How Moral Monday's 'Fusion Politics' Trumped North Carolina's Right-Wing Extremists and How They Will Continue to Do So," *First of the Month*, January 12, 2017, https://www.firstofthemonth.org/strategy-memo-ii-how-moral-mondays-fusion-politics-trumped -north-carolinas-right-wing-extremists-and-how-they-will-continue-to-do-so/.

Rev. William Barber, "Why We Are Here Today," NAACP of North Carolina, April 29, 2013, https://carolinajustice.typepad.com/ncnaacp/page/3/.

WRAL, "NC Voter ID Bill Moving Ahead with Supreme Court Ruling."

Spencer Lachmanec, "What the Hell is Happening in North Carolina?," *Rantt Media*, January 7, 2017, https://medium.com/rantt/what-the-hell-is-happening-in-north-carolina -4e0aef82eb14.

Shane Ryan, "Judges May Soon Rule on Future 10th and 11th Congressional Districts," *Carolina Public Press*, December 12, 2011, https://carolinapublicpress.org/8053/judges-expected -to-rule-on-future-10th-and-11th-congressional-districts-soon/.

Mosi Secret, "Firing Up the Faithful," *Indy Week*, February 1, 2006, https://indyweek.com/news/ firing-faithful/.

Emiene Wright, "William Barber, the Lightning Rod," *Creative Loafing*, December 25, 2013, https://clclt.com/charlotte/william-barber-the-lightning-rod/Content?oid=3287601.

Sue Sturgis, "Historic Progressive March Planned for North Carolina," *Facing South*, February 8, 2007, https://www.facingsouth.org/2007/02/historic-progressive-march-planned-for-north -carolina.html.

Jonathan Wilson-Hartgrove, "How William J. Barber Saved Wake County Schools," *Sojourners*, February 10, 2011, https://sojo.net/articles/how-william-j-barber-saved-wake-county-schools.

Rev. William Barber, "Wake Up! Voter Suppression is Not Dead," *Essence*, December 13, 2018, https://www.essence.com/news/politics/voter-suppression-is-not-dead/.

SNCC Digital Gateway, "Bob Zellner," https://snccdigital.org/people/bob-zellner/.

Ari Berman, "North Carolina's Moral Mondays," *The Nation*, July 17, 2013, https://www.thenation. com/article/archive/north-carolinas-moral-mondays/.

Jamie Fuller, "800,000 People Protested in North Carolina This Weekend," *Washington Post*, February 10, 2014, https://www.washingtonpost.com/news/the-fix/wp/2014/02/10/ why-tens-of-thousands-of-people-were-rallying-in-raleigh/.

Karen Garloch, "Charlotte-area Teen Ash Haffner Struggled with Gender Identity," *Charlotte Observer*, March 28, 2015, https://www.charlotteobserver.com/news/local/article16652432.html.

Karen Garloch, "Charlotte-area Transgender Teens' Suicides Rock Community," *Charlotte Observer*, March 28, 2015, https://www.charlotteobserver.com/news/local/article16655111.html.

Berman, Give Us the Ballot, 290.

Nichol, *Indecent Assembly*, 6, chap. 7.

CHAPTER 9

Billy Corriher and Sean Wright, "Keeping Campaign Cash Out of North Carolina's Courts," Center for American Progress, September 30, 2014, https://www.americanprogress.org/issues/courts/reports/2014/09/30/98121/keeping-campaign-cash-out-of-north-carolina-courts/.

Angie Newsome, "Poll: NC Voters Favor Judicial Public Financing," May 9, 2013, *Carolina Public Press*, https://carolinapublicpress.org/15218/poll-nc-voters-favor-judicial-public-financing/.

Brennan Center for Justice, "Buying Time: North Carolina 2012," October 19, 2012, https://www.brennancenter.org/our-work/research-reports/buying-time-2012-north-carolina.

National Institute on Money in State Politics, "Show Me Contributions to State Supreme Court Candidates in Elections in North Carolina 2012," accessed on March 2, 2021, https://www.followthemoney.org/show-me?s=NC&y=2012&c-r-ot=J&gro=c-t-id#%5B%7B1%7Cgro=c-t-id,d-eid.

Sue Sturgis, "Institute Index: Buying the Courts in North Carolina," *Facing South*, April 26, 2013, https://www.facingsouth.org/2013/04/institute-index-buying-the-courts-in-north-carolin.html.

Alan Suderman and Ben Weider, "Secret Money is Now Swaying State Judicial Elections," *Mother Jones*, June 13, 2013, https://www.motherjones.com/politics/2013/06/state-supreme-court-election-spending/.

Center for Responsive Politics, "Republican State Leadership Cmte: 2012," https://www.opensecrets.org/527s/527cmtedetail_contribs.php?cycle=2012&ein=050532524.

Billy Corriher, "Millionaire Campaign Donor Could Singlehandedly Kill North Carolina's Public Financing for Judicial Elections," *ThinkProgress*, June 20, 2013, https://thinkprogress.org/millionaire-campaign-donor-could-singlehandedly-kill-north-carolinas-public-financing-for-judicial-5e6710d31544/.

Melissa Kromm, interview by Billy Corriher. North Carolina, September 14, 2020.

Chris Kromm, interview by Chris Hayes. *All In with Chris Hayes*, June 17, 2013, https://www.nbcnews.com/id/wbna52230037.

N.C. General Assembly, *Voter Information Verification Act*.

Billy Corriher and Sean Wright, "Dirty Money, Dirty Water" (Washington, D.C.: Center for American Progress), 2014, https://cdn.americanprogress.org/wp-content/uploads/2014/11/DirtyMoneyDirtyWater-report.pdf.

Billy Corriher, "Big Business Taking Over State Supreme Courts" (Washington, D.C.: Center for American Progress), 2012, https://www.americanprogress.org/wp-content/uploads/2012/08/StateCourtsReport.pdf.

Editorial, "Judicial Elections and the Bottom Line," *New York Times*, August 19, 2012, https://www.nytimes.com/2012/08/20/opinion/judicial-elections-and-the-bottom-line.html.

Brennan Center for Justice, "Buying Time: North Carolina 2014," updated on November 16, 2014, https://www.brennancenter.org/our-work/research-reports/buying-time-2014-north-carolina.

Mark Binker, "Supreme Court Spending 'All About Redistricting,'" *WRAL*, updated July 18, 2018, https://www.wral.com/supreme-court-spending-all-about-redistricting-/16168892/.

CHAPTER 10

Daley, *Ratf**ked*, 19.

William Haltom and Michael McCann, *Distorting the Law: Politics, Media, and the Litigation Crisis* (Chicago: The University of Chicago Press, 2004), chap. 2-3.

Suderman and Weider, "Secret Money is Now Swaying State Judicial Elections."

Billy Corriher, "Voting Rights Advocates Turn to North Carolina Courts, Stacked by Campaign Cash," *Center for American Progress*, September 2, 2015, https://www.americanprogress.org/issues/courts/news/2015/09/02/120437/voting-rights-advocates-turn-to-north-carolina-courts-stacked-by-campaign-cash/.

Sharon McCloskey, "Groups Call on Newby to Recuse Himself in Redistricting Dispute," *NC Policy Watch*, November 21, 2012, http://www.ncpolicywatch.com/2012/11/21/groups-call-on-newby-to-recuse-himself-in-redistricting-dispute/

Plaintiff-Appellants' Motion for Recusal of Justice Paul Newby, *Dickson v. Rucho*, 367 N.C. 542, October 11, 2013, https://www.ncappellatecourts.org/show-file.php?document_id=146270.

Legislative Defendants' Response to Plaintiff-Appellants' Motion for Recusal of Justice Paul Newby, *Dickson v. Rucho*, 367 N.C. 542, December 3, 2012, https://archive.org/stream/540997-farr-response-to-newby-recusal-motion/540997-farr-response-to-newby-recusal-motion_djvu.txt.

Supreme Court of North Carolina to Edwin Speas, "RE: Dickson, et al v Rucho, et al – 201PA12-1," December 17, 2012, http://pulse.ncpolicywatch.org/wp-content/uploads/2015/08/Newby-recusal.pdf.

Chris Jankowski to Legislative Leaders, https://www.documentcloud.org/documents/537408-hofeller-sglf-rslc-letter.

Sharon McCloskey, "Behind Closed Doors: North Carolina Creates a Star Chamber for Wayward Judges," *NC Policy Watch*, July 31, 2013, http://www.ncpolicywatch.com/2013/07/31/behind-closed-doors-north-carolina-creates-a-star-chamber-for-wayward-judges/.

Tom Bullock, "Record Campaign Cash for Judges, But Are There Rules to Keep Justice Fair?" *WFAE*, May 16, 2014, https://www.wfae.org/local-news/2014-05-16/record-campaign-cash-for-judges-but-are-there-rules-to-keep-justice-fair.

Jordan Green and Chad Nance, "Republican Lawmakers Exert Control over Local Courts," *Triad City Beat*, August 6, 2014, http://www.camelcitydispatch.com/republican-lawmakers-exert-control-over-local-courts-6874/.

Laura Leslie, "Senate GOP Seeks to Sweep Oversight Boards," *WRAL*, February 5, 2013, https://www.wral.com/senate-gop-seeks-to-sweep-oversight-boards-/12066869/.

Sharon McCloskey, "Win the Courts, Win the War: How the State Supreme Court Advanced the Conservative Agenda," *NC Policy Watch*, December 15, 2015, http://www.ncpolicywatch.com/2015/12/15/win-the-courts-win-the-war/.

Rob Schofield, "Lack of Diversity Continues to Plague the North Carolina General Assembly," *NC Policy Watch*, January 9, 2015, http://pulse.ncpolicywatch.org/2015/01/09/lack-of-diversity-continues-to-plague-general-assembly/#sthash.42Zz1qBj.KJc8EwCR.dpbs.

CHAPTER 11

Pema Levy, "A Judicial Election Threatened North Carolina Republicans' Agenda. So They Canceled the Election," *Mother Jones*, June 18, 2015, https://www.motherjones.com/politics/2015/06/north-carolina-republicans-judicial-election/.

Melissa Kromm, "Judicial Reform Farce May Put NC Supreme Court in a Pickle," *News Observer*, March 18, 2016, https://www.newsobserver.com/opinion/op-ed/article66015042.html.

Lynn Bonner, "Bill Would Change State Judicial Elections," *News Observer*, April 20, 2015, https://www.newsobserver.com/news/politics-government/politics-columns-blogs/under-the-dome/article19084023.html.

Chris Fitzsimon, "The Most Important Court Case Last Week had Nothing to do With Gerrymandering," *NC Policy Watch*, February 23, 2016, http://www.ncpolicywatch.com/2016/02/23/the-most-important-court-case-last-week-had-nothing-to-do-with-redistricting/.

Faires v. Board of Elections, No. 15-CVS-15903, March 4, 2015, https://electionlawblog.org/wp-content/uploads/Retention-Election-Order-of-Three-Judge-Panel.pdf.

Fairies v. Board of Elections, No. 84A16, May 6, 2016, https://appellate.nccourts.org/opinions/?c=1&pdf=34331.

CHAPTER 12

Anita Earls, interview by Billy Corriher. North Carolina, September 14, 2020.

H. Philip West, "Secrets and Scandals: Reforming Rhode Island, 1986-2006, Chapter 40," *Go Local Prov*, December 7, 2015, https://www.golocalprov.com/news/secrets-and-scandals-reforming-rhode-island-1986-2006-chapter-40.

Anne Blythe and Bryan Murphy, "3 Trump Judicial Nominees Out. Now Another Faces Scrutiny About Work for Jesse Helms," *News Observer*, December 22, 2017, https://www.newsobserver.com/news/politics-government/state-politics/article191254104.html.

"Groups Pushing for more African Americans on Courts," *Ballotpedia*, November 7, 2011, https://ballotpedia.org/Groups_pushing_for_more_African-Americans_on_courts.

NAACP, "Watch NAACP President Derrick Johnson Speak Out Against Thomas Farr," https://fb.watch/3_FoAroFYb/.

"Thomas Farr Confirmation Hearing," *C-SPAN*, September 20, 2017, https://www.c-span.org/video/?c4761111/thomas-farr-confrimation-hearing.

Billy Corriher, "GOP Seeks Judges Who Will Stifle Voting Rights," September 22, 2017, *News Observer*, https://www.newsobserver.com/opinion/op-ed/article174851586.html.

Julyssa Lopez, "Kamala Harris and Cory Booker Become First Black Members of the Senate Judiciary Committee This Century," *Glamour*, January 10, 2018, https://www.glamour.com/story/kamala-harris-cory-booker-first-black-members-senate-judiciary-committee-this-century.

Leslie Proll, "Trump and the Courts: Bias on the Bench," *The Crisis*, September 4, 2018, https://www.thecrisismagazine.com/single-post/2018/09/04/Bias-On-The-Bench.

CHAPTER 13

Ken Fine, "How Did Mike Morgan Win?" *Indy Week*, November 23, 2016, https://indyweek.com/news/mike-morgan-win/.

Rev. William Barber, "The 11th Annual Moral March on Raleigh and HKonJ People's Assembly," February 11, 2017, https://www.facebook.com/434927366627142/videos/1557120784407789.

Billy Corriher, "North Carolina's Legislature has a Devious Plan to Overturn the Will of the Voters," *ThinkProgress*, November 15, 2016, https://thinkprogress.org/north-carolina -supreme-court-33e0873acb30/.

Mitch Kokai, "Legislature Could Counteract Supreme Court Election Result by Expanding High Court," *Carolina Journal*, November 10, 2016, https://www.carolinajournal.com/news-article/legislature-could-counteract-supreme-court-election-result-by-expanding -high-court/.

Editorial, "If You Can't Win the Court, Stack it," *Wilmington Star News*, November 11, 2016, https://www.starnewsonline.com/opinion/20161120/editorial-nov-20-if-you -cant-win-court-stack-it.

Rob Schofield, "Court Packing Move Would Set a Dangerous New Low for NC GOP," *NC Policy Watch*, November 11, 2016, http://pulse.ncpolicywatch.org/2016/11/11/court-packing-move -set-new-low-nc-gop/.

Melissa Boughton, "Justice-elect Mike Morgan Weighs in on Supreme Court Win, Rumors of Court Packing," *NC Policy Watch*, November 23, 2016, http://pulse.ncpolicywatch.org/2016/11/23/justice -elect-mike-morgan-weighs-supreme-court-win-rumors-court-packing/.

"NAACP Will Sue if Republicans Pursue 'Court Packing' of Supreme Court," *News Observer*, November 20, 2016, https://greensboro.com/z-no-digital/naacp-will-sue-if-republicans-pursue -court-packing-of-supreme/article_030339c0-6196-5c17-bb72-2479cc5d70df.html.

Melissa Boughton, "GOP Legislative Leaders Could Make Rare Court Packing Move to Keep Partisan Control of State Supreme Court," *NC Policy Watch*, November 11, 2016, http://www.ncpolicywatch.com/2016/11/11/gop-legislative-leaders-make-rare-court-packing-move -keep-partisan-control-state-supreme-court/.

Frank Taboni, "Reality Check: North Carolina Supreme Court Packing," *WLOS*, November 29, 2016, https://wlos.com/news/reality-check/stacking-north-carolina-supreme-court.

Albert Hunt, "North Carolina Republicans Wants to Rig the System," *Bloomberg*, December 7, 2016, https://www.bloombergquint.com/opinion/north-carolina-republicans -want-to-rig-the-system.

Alice Olstein, "North Carolina GOP Rams Through Bill Giving Itself More Power in All Election Years," *ThinkProgress*, December 16, 2016, https://archive.thinkprogress.org/north-carolina-gop-power-election-years-1a10437c8f8b/.

David Graham, "North Carolina Republicans' Bid to Snatch the Governor's Power," *The Atlantic*, December 14, 2016, https://www.theatlantic.com/politics/archive/2016/12/north-carolina-special-session-republicans-roy-cooper/510731/.

Billy Corriher, "North Carolina Legislature Attempting Virtual Coup of New Democratic Governor," *ThinkProgress*, December 15, 2016, https://thinkprogress.org/north -carolina-legislature-dem-governor-b2298c8d7509/.

Drew Millard, "Inside the Republican Power Grab in North Carolina," *VICE*, December 16, 2016, https://www.vice.com/en/article/qkbnjw/republican-power-grab-north-carolina.

Joe Killian, "General Assembly Moves to Dramatically Limit New Governor's Powers, *NC Policy Watch*, December 14, 2016, http://pulse.ncpolicywatch.org/2016/12/14/general-assembly-moves-dramatically-limit-new-governors-powers/.

Purdy, "North Carolina's Partisan Crisis."

"Cooper Pushes Back Against Legislative Move to Limit His Powers," *Charlotte Observer*, December 15, 2016, https://www.charlotteobserver.com/news/politics-government/article121225408.html.

Greg Bluestein, "N.C. Governor Signs Measure to Curb Powers of His Democratic Successor," *Atlanta-Journal Constitution*, December 16, 2016, https://www.ajc.com/blog/politics/governor-signs-measure-curb-powers-his-democratic-successor/4s02LpwDBgmMe50Jd5PaiO/.

Joe Killian, "Did Gov. McCrory Battle Court Packing Scheme, or Was it a Media Myth?" *NC Policy Watch*, December 19, 2016, http://pulse.ncpolicywatch.org/2016/12/19/gov-mccrory-battle-court-packing-scheme-media-myth/.

Sophia Tesfaye, "Ousted North Carolina GOP Governor Curtails Successor's Powers Amidst Republican Assault on Power," *Salon*, December 16, 2016, https://www.salon.com/2016/12/16/ousted-north-carolina-gop-governor-curtails-sucessors-powers-amidst-republican-assault-on-power/.

Steven Porter, "N.C. Republican Lawmakers Scramble to Weaken Incoming Governor's Power," *Christian Science Monitor*, December 15, 2016, https://www.csmonitor.com/USA/Politics/2016/1215/N.C.-Republican-lawmakers-scramble-to-weaken-incoming-governor-s-power.

Melissa Boughton, "Good Concepts or Bad – Experts Say Politicizing the Courts in Special Session Detrimental to Judicial Independence, Public Perception," *NC Policy Watch*, December 20, 2016, http://www.ncpolicywatch.com/2016/12/20/good-concepts-bad-experts-say-politicizing-courts-special-session-detrimental-judicial-independence-public-perception/.

Southern Coalition for Social Justice, "NC Legislative Rewrite Undermines Democratic Principles," SCSJ press release, December 14, 2016 https://southerncoalition.org/9029-2/.

CHAPTER 14

"Election 2014: Beyond the Horserace," *ThinkProgress*, November 2, 2014, https://archive.thinkprogress.org/election-2014-beyond-the-horserace-97569f11fee2/.

Michael Wines, "Critics Say North Carolina Is Curbing Black Vote. Again," *New York Times*, August 31, 2016, https://www.nytimes.com/2016/08/31/us/politics/election-rules-north-carolina.html?_r=1.

"Full Email Sent by Dallas Woodhouse," *WRAL*, August 17, 2016, https://www.wral.com/full-email-sent-by-dallas-woodhouse/15938449/.

Max Rosenthal, "North Carolina GOP Brags About How Few Black People Were Able to Vote Early," *Mother Jones*, November 7, 2016, https://www.motherjones.com/politics/2016/11/north-carolina-gop-brags-about-how-few-black-people-were-able-vote-early/.

North Carolina Republican Party, "NCGOP Sees Encouraging Early Voting, Obama/Clinton Coalition Tired, Fail to Resonate in North Carolina," NC GOP press release, November 6, 2016, https://us2.campaign-archive.com/?u=f3100bc5464cbba2f472ddf2c&id=e4b9a8fb19.

Anne Blythe, "Josh Stein Lays Off Employees After $10 Million Cuts," *News Observer*, August 3, 2017, https://www.newsobserver.com/news/politics-government/state-politics/article165172877.html.

Anne Blythe, "Roy Cooper Challenges NC GOP's Elections Board Makeover," *News Observer*, December 30, 2016, https://www.newsobserver.com/news/politics-government/state-politics/article123763694.html.

Melissa Boughton, "Three-Judge Panel Temporarily Blocks Law Overhauling State Elections Board," *NC Policy Watch*, January 6, 2017, http://pulse.ncpolicywatch.org/2017/01/06/three-judge-panel-temporarily-blocks-law-overhauling-state-board-elections/.

Melissa Boughton, "Three-Judge Panels to Hear Constitutional Arguments on Laws Passed by Republican Legislature in Surprise Special Session," *NC Policy Watch*, January 5, 2017, http://www.ncpolicywatch.com/2017/01/05/three-judge-panels-hear-constitutional-arguments-laws-passed-republican-legislature-surprise-special-session/.

Cooper v. Berger, 809 S.E.2d 98 (N.C. 2018), https://law.justia.com/cases/north-carolina/supreme-court/2018/52pa17-2.html.

Tae Aderman, "North Carolina Courts Again Strike Down Chair Selection Process for New State Ethics Board," *Multistate*, November 26, 2018, https://www.multistate.us/insider/2018/11/26/north-carolina-courts-again-strike-down-chair-selection-process-for-new-state-ethics-board.

Mark Joseph Stern, " The North Carolina Supreme Court Just Blocked Republicans' Unlawful Election Board Power Grab," *Slate*, February 14, 2017, https://slate.com/news-and-politics/2017/02/north-carolina-supreme-court-blocks-republican-election-board-overhaul.html.

Associated Press, "Judges Block North Carolina Law Limiting Governor's Power Over Elections," *WITN*, February 8, 2017, https://www.witn.com/content/news/Judges-block-North-Carolina-law-limiting-governors-powers-413168763.html.

Associated Press, "Judges Hear Arguments over Restricting North Carolina Governor's Powers," *Los Angeles Times*, February 11, 2017, https://www.latimes.com/nation/nationnow/la-na-north-carolina-governor-20170211-story.html.

Phil Berger, "Legislative Leaders to Activist Judges: If You Want to Make Laws, Run for the Legislature," press release, Sen. Phil Berger, February 7, 2017, https://www.philberger.org/legislative_leaders_to_activist_judges_if_you_want_to_make_laws_run_for_the_legislature.

Anne Blythe, "N.C. Judges Reject Roy Cooper's Request to Block Cabinet Confirmation," *News Observer*, February 14, 2017, https://www.courier-tribune.com/news/20170214/nc-judges-reject-cooper8217s-request-to-block-cabinet-confirmation-process.

CHAPTER 15

Reply in Support of Petition for a Writ of Certiorari, *North Carolina v. North Carolina NAACP*, 581 U. S., 2017, https://www.brennancenter.org/sites/default/files/analysis/Reply_Brief_for_Petitioners_North_Carolina_02_13_17.pdf.

NAACP v. McCrory, 182 F.Supp.3d 320 (M.D.N.C. 2016).

Milca P., "Court Blocks North Carolina ID Law that Disenfranchised Black Voters," *The Source*, July 30, 2016, https://thesource.com/2016/07/30/court-blocks-north-carolina-id-law-that-disenfranchised-black-voters/.

U.S. Supreme Court, "Order List: 580 U.S.," May 15, 2017, https://www.supremecourt.gov/orders/courtorders/051517zor_986b.pdf.

Richard Wolf, "Supreme Court Strikes Down More North Carolina Election Districts," *USA Today*, June 15, 2017, https://www.usatoday.com/story/news/politics/2017/06/05/supreme-court-strikes-down-more-north-carolina-election-districts/102512186/.

Michael Wines, "North Carolina Republicans are Back with a New Plan for Strict Voting Laws," *New York Times*, June 15, 2018, https://www.nytimes.com/2018/06/15/us/north-carolina-voting-rights.html.

CHAPTER 16

Robert Hunter, interview by Billy Corriher. North Carolina, August 7, 2020.

Hunter, *Racial Gerrymandering and the Voting Rights Act in North Carolina.*

Republican Party of North Carolina v. Martin, 980 F.2d 943 (4th Cir. 1992).

Billy Corriher, "GOP Judge in North Carolina Resigns to Prevent 'Court Unpacking' by Legislature," *ThinkProgress*, April 24, 2017, https://thinkprogress.org/north-carolina-gop-judge-resigns-1559cf0dbb8c/.

Melissa Boughton, "An In-Depth Look at N.C. Lawmakers' Attempt to Shrink the Court of Appeals," *NC Policy Watch*, March 16, 2017, http://www.ncpolicywatch.com/2017/03/16/depth-look-n-c-lawmakers-attempt-shrink-court-appeals/.

Anne Blythe, "Courts and Judges: NC Republicans Push Partisan Judicial," *News Observer*, August 22, 2017, https://amp.newsobserver.com/news/politics-government/state-politics/article168661047.html.

Doug Clark, "Appeals Court Keeps 15 Judges with Timely Retirement, Appointment," *News Record*, April 24, 2017, https://greensboro.com/blogs/clark_off_the_record/appeals-court-keeps-judges-with-timely-retirement-appointment/article_642af482-2901-11e7-a951-33d7a2951509.html.

David Mildenberg, "Judges, Rep. Burr Clash over Election Districts," *Business North Carolina*, August 9, 2017, https://businessnc.com/judges-rep-burr-clash-election-districts/.

Billy Corriher, "NC Must Say No to Partisan Court Races," *News Observer*, February 24, 2015, https://www.newsobserver.com/opinion/op-ed/article11309846.html.

Trip Gabriel, "In North Carolina, Republicans Stung by Court Rulings Aim to Change the Judges," *New York Times*, October 18, 2017, https://www.nytimes.com/2017/10/18/us/north-carolina-republicans-gerrymander-judges-.html.

Editorial, "Republicans Politicizing State Courts," *Star News*, October 21, 2017, https://www.starnewsonline.com/opinion/20171021/editorial-oct-21-republicans-politicizing-state-courts.

Editorial, "Legislative Leaders Want to Put Justice Up for Sale," *WRAL*, October 20, 2017, https://www.wral.com/editorial-legislative-leaders-want-to-put-justice-up-for-sale/17030159/.

Ari Berman, "Courts Keep Thwarting North Carolina Republicans. So They're Trying to Remake the Courts," *Mother Jones*, January 23, 2018, https://www.motherjones.com/politics/2018/01/courts-keep-thwarting-north-carolina-republicans-so-theyre-trying-to-remake-the-courts/.

Marcia Morey, "Legislative Leaders Making Power Grab to Control NC Courts," *WRAL*, October 21, 2017, https://www.wral.com/marcia-morey-legislative-leaders-making-power-grab-to-control-n-c-courts/17032573/.

Matthew Burns, "Lawmakers Play Beat the Clock," *WRAL*, April 27, 2017, https://www.wral.com/lawmakers-play-beat-the-clock/16667127/.

Baker v. Martin, 410 S.E.2d 887 (N.C. 1991).

Nichol, *Indecent Assembly*, 120.

Paul Blest, "The North Carolina GOP's Campaign to Rig the Judiciary," *Scalawag*, September 7, 2017, https://scalawagmagazine.org/2017/09/the-north-carolina-gops-campaign-to-rig-the-judiciary/.

Alan Greenblatt, "Democratic Norms are Under Attack, and Not Just by Trump," *Governing*, May 18, 2017, https://www.governing.com/archive/gov-democracy-trump-states-legislatures.html.

Barry Yeoman, "The North Carolina GOP is Trying Every Trick to Keep a Supreme Court Seat," *Talking Points Memo*, October 18, 2018, https://talkingpointsmemo.com/feature/the-north-carolina-gop-is-trying-every-trick-to-keep-a-supreme-court-seat.

Kromm, interview.

CHAPTER 17

Justin Burr (@RepJustinBurr), "Attached are the maps for the PCS to HB 717 which will be heard tomorrow at 4 pm in Judiciary 1. #ncleg #ncpol," Twitter, June 25, 2017, https://twitter.com/RepJustinBurr/status/879145937830117376?s=20.

Billy Corriher, "North Carolina Republicans Look to Keep Power by Gerrymandering the Courts," *ThinkProgress*, June 26, 2017, https://thinkprogress.org/north-carolina-legislature-looks-to-keep-power-by-gerrymandering-courts-9a6376fb52c8/.

Alicia Bannon and Nathaniel Sobel, " Assaults on the Courts: Legislative Roundup," Brennan Center for Justice, May 8, 2017, https://www.brennancenter.org/our-work/research-reports/assaults-courts-legislative-round.

German Lopez, "Charlotte Police Officer Who Shot and Killed Keith Lamont Scott Will not Face Charges," *Vox*, November 30, 2016, https://www.vox.com/2016/9/21/12999366/keith-lamont-scott-north-carolina-police-shooting.

Melissa Boughton, "ICYMI: Mecklenburg District Judges Speak Out Against Lawmakers' Effort to Subdivide Court Districts," *NC Policy Watch*, March 28, 2017, http://pulse.ncpolicywatch.org/2017/03/28/icymi-mecklenburg-district-judges-speak-lawmakers-effort-subdivide-court-districts/.

Erica Hellerstein, "Over Accusations of Gerrymandering, Republicans Introduce Bill to Redraw Judicial Maps," *Indy Week*, June 27, 2017, https://indyweek.com/news/archives/accusations-gerrymandering-republicans-introduce-bill-redraw-judicial-maps/.

John Hood, (@JohnHoodNC), "It's clear that North Carolina must redraw its judicial districts. Former General Assembly lawyer Gerry Cohen argues, for example, that a lawsuit against Mecklenburg County's districts alone would likely win on summary judgment. https://buff.ly/2B3GEBX #ncpol #ncga," Twitter, November 20, 2017, https://twitter.com/JohnHoodNC/status/932611491420889088?s=20.

Mildenberg, "Judges, Rep. Burr Clash over Election Districts."

Marcia Morey, "Justice in North Carolina Under Attack," *Durham Herald-Sun*, September 13, 2017, https://www.heraldsun.com/opinion/article172241102.html.

Hellerstein, "Over Accusations of Gerrymandering, Republicans Introduce Bill to Redraw Judicial Maps."

"Redistricting Brief: Gerrymandered Courts Bill Favors Republicans in Superior Court," Real Facts NC, September 29, 2017, https://nmcdn.io/e186d21f8c7946a19faed23c3da2f0da/7c49efad-c86e4da38d1ad3086f727890/files/20170927_judicial-redistricting-report.pdf.

Laura Leslie, "House Panel OKs New Judicial Election Districts," WRAL, updated July 13, 2018, https://www.wral.com/house-panel-oks-new-judicial-districts/16978070/.

Blest, "The North Carolina GOP's Campaign to Rig the Judiciary."

Melissa Boughton, " GOP Plan to Redistrict Judges in Mecklenburg Wins Quick Senate Approval; Dems, Judges Cry Foul," NC Policy Watch, May 31, 2018, http://www.ncpolicywatch.com/2018/05/31/gop-plan-to-redistrict-judges-in-mecklenburg-wins-quick-senate-approval-dems-judges-cry-foul/.

Kirk Ross, "Major NC Judicial District Reshuffling Moves Forward," Carolina Public Press, September 22, 2017, https://carolinapublicpress.org/27479/major-judicial-district-reshuffling-moves-forward/.

Anne Blythe and Greg Jarvis, "Judge, DA Districts Targeted in Redistricting Plan," News Observer, June 26, 2017, http://www.newsobserver.com/news/politics-government/state-politics/article158264799.html.

Gabriel, "In North Carolina, Republicans Stung by Court Rulings Aim to Change the Judges."

"Judicial Redistricting in North Carolina: A Plan for Second Class Justice," Southern Coalition for Social Justice, March 20, 2018, https://southerncoalition.org/wp-content/uploads/2019/02/SCSJ-Judicial-Redistricting-Analysis-FINAL-rev.-3-20-18.pdf.

Melissa Boughton, "Policy Watch Exclusive: Double-Bunked Judges Speak out on Judicial Redistricting Plans," NC Policy Watch, April 26, 2018, http://www.ncpolicywatch.com/2018/04/26/policy-watch-exclusive-double-bunked-judges-speak-out-on-judicial-redistricting-plans/.

"House Roll Call Vote #945," North Carolina General Assembly, October 5, 2017, https://www.ncleg.gov/Legislation/Votes/RollCallVoteTranscript/2017/H/945.

CHAPTER 18

Kimberly Best, Interview by Billy Corriher, Phone interview, September 15, 2020.

Boughton, "GOP Plan to Redistrict Judges in Mecklenburg Wins Quick Senate Approval; Dems, Judges Cry Foul."

Jim Morrill, "Judges in Mecklenburg Judicial Districts Scrambling Days Before Election Filing," WBTV, November 28, 2019, https://www.wbtv.com/2019/11/28/judges-mecklenburg-judicial-districts-scrambling-days-before-election-filing/.

Mildenberg, "Judges, Rep. Burr Clash over Election Districts."

Melissa Boughton, "NC Courts Commission Recommends Lawmakers Hold off On Judicial Redistricting until Next Year," NC Policy Watch, September 29, 2017, http://pulse.ncpolicywatch.org/2017/09/29/nc-courts-commission-recommends-lawmakers-hold-off-judicial-redistricting-next-year/.

Billy Corriher, "North Carolina Gerrymandering Bill Pits Black Judges Against Other Incumbents," ThinkProgress, October 6, 2017, https://thinkprogress.org/judicial-gerrymandering-north-carolina-56f15b92f01f/.

Melissa Boughton, " A Guide to Proposed Judicial Maps as Court Commission Set to Meet Today," *NC Policy Watch*, September 29, 2017, http://pulse.ncpolicywatch.org/2017/09/29/guide-proposed -judicial-maps-court-commission-set-meet-today/.

Billy Corriher (@billycorriher), "The #HofellerFiles are out! For real this time. http://thehofellerfiles. com I found this map of judicial election districts in Charlotte, NC, which were redrawn by #NCGA in 2017. It includes a breakdown of previous GOP votes," Twitter, January 5, 2020, https://twitter. com/BillyCorriher/status/1213945621444468736?s=20.

Billy Corriher, "Voting Rights Lawsuits Aim to Foster Judicial Diversity Across the South," *Facing South*, February 22, 2018, https://www.facingsouth.org/2018/02/voting-rights -lawsuits-aim-foster-judicial-diversity-across-south.

Melissa Boughton, "Stealth Session? G.A. Returns Today, But the Agenda (Including Plans for Judicial Redistricting) Remains Under Wraps," *NC Policy Watch*, May 26, 2018, http://www. ncpolicywatch.com/2018/05/16/stealth-session-g-a-returns-today-but-the-agenda-including -plans-for-judicial-redistricting-remains-under-wraps/.

Melissa Boughton, " Lewis: Statewide Judicial Redistricting Off the Table this Session," *NC Policy Watch*, June 6, 2018, http://pulse.ncpolicywatch.org/2018/06/02/lewis-statewide-judicial -redistricting-off-the-table-this-session/.

"2018 Election Results," *Charlotte Observer*, November 7, 2018, https://www.charlotteobserver. com/news/politics-government/election/article221036810.html.

CHAPTER 19

Anne Blythe, "'North Carolina is a Test Case, Y'all," *News Observer*, January 10, 2018, https://www. newsobserver.com/news/politics-government/state-politics/article193988424.html.

Jordan Green, "Citizen Green: As Legislative Maps Fail, GOP on to Judiciary," *Triad City Beat*, January 19, 2018, https://triad-city-beat.com/legislative-maps-fail-nc-gop-moves-judiciary/.

William Barber to U.S. Senate Judiciary Committee, January 18, 2018, https://medium.com/ brepairers/opposition-to-the-re-nomination-of-thomas-farr-to-the-federal-judiciary- dc2802d4e602.

Clarissa Hamlin, "Not Today, Not Ever: Black Folks Protest Thomas Farr's Lifetime Judicial Nomination," *NewsOne*, April 4, 2018, https://newsone.com/3788084/thomas-farr -nomination-judge-controversy-protest-naacp-ldf/amp/.

William Barber, "Kavanaugh on the Supreme Court Would Endanger Rights of Women, Workers & Voters." Interview by Amy Goodman. *War and Peace Report*, Democracy Now, September 19, 2018, https://www.democracynow.org/2018/9/19/rev_william_barber_kavanaugh_on_the.

Tara Golshan, "Did Brett Kavanaugh Perjure Himself During His Confirmation Hearing?," *Vox*, September 15, 2019, https://www.vox.com/policy-and-politics/2019/9/15/20866829/ brett-kavanaugh-perjury-confirmation-hearing-deborah-ramirez-new-allegations.

CHAPTER 20

Earls, interview.

Complaint, *League of Women Voters v. Rucho*, 1:16-CV-1164, N.C. Super. Ct., September 22, 2016, https://www.brennancenter.org/sites/default/files/legal-work/Plaintiffs%27%20Complaint.pdf.

League of Women Voters of North Carolina Plaintiffs' Final Proposed Findings of Fact and Conclusions of Law, *Common Cause v. Rucho*, 279 F.Supp.3d 587, November 6, 2017, https://www. brennancenter.org/sites/default/files/legal-work/CC_LWV_v_Rucho_LWVNC-Plaintiffs-Final-Proposed-Findings-of-Fact-and-Conclusions-of-Law.compressed.pdf.

Legislative Defendants Proposed Findings of Fact and Conclusions of Law, *Common Cause v. Rucho*, 279 F.Supp.3d 587, November 6, 2017, https://www.brennancenter.org/sites/default/files/legal-work/CC_LWV_v_Rucho_Legislative-Defendants-Proposed-Findings-of-Fact-and-Conclusions-of-Law.pdf.

Amy Howe, "Argument Analysis: Justices Divided and Hard to Read on Partisan Gerrymandering," *SCOTUSblog*, March 26, 2019, https://www.scotusblog.com/2019/03/argument-analysis-justices-divided-and-hard-to-read-on-partisan-gerrymandering/.

Rucho v. Common Cause, 139 S.Ct. 2484 (2019).

Will Doran, "Democrats Think They Can Flip a Key Seat on the N.C. Supreme Court. Here are the Candidates.," *News Observer*, October 20, 2018, https://greensboro.com/ap/north_carolina/democrats-think-they-can-flip-a-key-seat-on-the-n-c-supreme-court-here/article_77f6a4e0-9e02-542d-add0-a741cc5149f6.html.

Barry Yeoman, "The North Carolina GOP Is Trying Every Trick To Keep A Supreme Court Seat," *Talking Points Memo*, October 18, 2018, https://talkingpointsmemo.com/feature/the-north-carolina-gop-is-trying-every-trick-to-keep-a-supreme-court-seat.

CHAPTER 22

"S.C. Supreme Court Elections—Quick and Quiet," South Carolina Policy Council, February 6, 2018, http://scpolicycouncil.org/research/who-picks-judges-in-south-carolina.

Melissa Boughton, "Merit or Maps? Judges' Futures Could Come Down to Clashing Legislative Proposals," *NC Policy Watch*, August 15, 2017, http://www.ncpolicywatch.com/2017/08/15/merit-maps-judges-futures-come-clashing-legislative-proposals/.

Rebekah Barber and Billy Corriher, "Honoring Reconstruction's Legacy: The Freedom to Vote," *Facing South*, September 13, 2018, https://www.facingsouth.org/2018/09/honoring-reconstructions-legacy-freedom-vote.

Ned Barnette, "An Independent Judiciary is Under Siege in Washington and N.C.," *News Observer*, November 25, 2017, http://www.newsobserver.com/opinion/editorials/article186355103.html.

"After Republican Leaders Refuse to Allow Retired Judge to Speak on Judicial Redistricting, Democrats Walk Out in Protest," *Real Facts NC*, December 14, 2017, https://realfactsnc.com/blog/after-republican-leaders-refuse-to-allow-retired-judge-to-speak-on-judicial-redistricting-democrats-walk-out-in-protest.

Melissa Boughton, "Could Judicial Reform Lead to Supreme Court Packing? Former Judge Thinks So," *NC Policy Watch*, January 18, 2018, http://www.ncpolicywatch.com/2018/01/18/judicial-reform-lead-supreme-court-packing-former-judge-thinks/.

Liz Schlemmer, "Judicial Vacancy Amendment Heading to North Carolina Voters," *WUNC*, June 28, 2018, https://www.wunc.org/post/judicial-vacancy-amendment-heading-north-carolina-voters.

Will Rierson, "Debate Highlights Partisan Divide on Judicial-Vacancies Amendment," *Warren Record*, September 27, 2018, https://www.warrenrecord.com/news/article_d3162622-c24e-11e8-9b1f-1f366ddd65d8.html.

Melissa Boughton, "NCGA Wants Power to Appoint Judicial Vacancies as Alternative Merit Selection," *NC Policy Watch*, April 27, 2018, http://pulse.ncpolicywatch.org/2018/04/27/ncga-wants-power-to-appoint-judicial-vacancies-as-alternative-merit-selection/.

Melissa Boughton, "Senate Passes Victims' Rights, Judicial Vacancy Selection Constitutional Amendments," *NC Policy Watch*, June 26, 2018, http://pulse.ncpolicywatch.org/2018/06/26/senate-passes-victims-rights-judicial-vacancy-selection-constitutional-amendments/.

Melissa Boughton, "Merit Selection Still Cloaked in Secrecy as Senate Committee Takes on 'Judicial Reform,'" *NC Policy Watch*, November 9, 2017, http://www.ncpolicywatch.com/2017/11/09/merit-selection-still-cloaked-secrecy-senate-committee-takes-judicial-reform/.

Melissa Boughton, "Expert: Judicial Selection Plan 'Window Dressing' for Legislative Appointments," *NC Policy Watch*, January 4, 2018, http://pulse.ncpolicywatch.org/2018/01/04/expert-judicial-selection-plan-window-dressing-legislative-appointments/.

Paul Woolverton, "Protesters Rally Against Possible Cancellation of Judge Elections," *Fayetteville Observer*, January 9, 2018, https://www.fayobserver.com/news/20180109/protesters-rally-against-possible-cancellation-of-judge-elections.

CHAPTER 23

Rep. David Lewis to Sen. Tim Moore, July 21, 2018, http://www.ncpolicywatch.com/wp-content/uploads/2018/07/David-Lewis-letter.pdf.

Billy Ball, "State Lawmakers Move to Seize Power over Constitutional Amendment Captions," *NC Policy Watch*, July 24, 2018, http://pulse.ncpolicywatch.org/2018/07/24/state-lawmakers-move-to-seize-power-over-constitutional-amendment-captions/.

Billy Corriher, "North Carolina Republicans 'Rig the System' by Cancelling 2018 Judicial Elections," *ThinkProgress*, October 17, 2017, https://archive.thinkprogress.org/north-carolina-legislature-cancel-judicial-elections-34f78d9d6669/.

Laura Leslie, "Impeachment of Justices Possible, GOP Chief Says," *WRAL*, August 17, 2018, https://www.wral.com/impeachment-of-justices-possible-gop-chief-says/17776194/.

Complaint, *Cooper v. Berger*, 18 CVS ___, N.C. Super. Ct. August 4, 2018, https://www.courthousenews.com/wp-content/uploads/2018/08/Cooper-complaint.pdf.

N.C. General Assembly, House, *An Act to Amend the North Carolina Constitution*, HB 3, 2018, 2nd extra sess., https://www.ncleg.net/Sessions/2017E2/Bills/House/PDF/H3v4.pdf.

Kirk Ross, "NC's Battle for Regulatory Control," *Coastal Review Online*, July 2, 2018, https://www.coastalreview.org/2018/07/analysis-ncs-battle-for-regulatory-control/.

Kirk Ross, "On the Ballot this Fall, an Historic Power Struggle," *Coastal Review Online*, August 15, 2018, https://www.coastalreview.org/2018/07/analysis-ncs-battle-for-regulatory-control/.

Editorial, "Our View: The Legislature's Power Grab," *Winston-Salem Journal*, July 12, 2018, https://journalnow.com/opinion/editorials/our-view-the-legislature-s-power-grab/article_63671d3b-d5d0-5e6f-a057-e5f4a015ef1a.amp.html.

Cooper v. Berger, 772 S.E.2d 80 (N.C. 2015).

Editorial, "Special Session Reveals Phony Motives Behind Constitutional Amendments," *WRAL*, July 23, 2018, https://www.wral.com/editorial-special-session-reveals-phony-motives-behind-constitutional-amendments/17714739/.

Julia Harte, "Insight: Emails Show how Republicans Lobbied to Limit Voting Hours in North Carolina," *Reuters*, November 3, 2016, https://www.reuters.com/article/us-usa-election-northcarolina-insight/insight-emails-show-how-republicans-lobbied-to-limit-voting-hours-in-north-carolina-idUSKBN12Y0ZY.

Billy Corriher (@BillyCorriher), "Rep. Jackson (D) asks if an even-numbered Elections Board would be more likely to have tie votes than an odd-numbered Board. Rep. Torbett (R-Gaston) says 'no.' Wow…. #nixallsix #ncga," Twitter, August 24, 2018, https://twitter.com/BillyCorriher/status/1033022609267609600?s=20.

Billy Corriher, "Ballot Changes Cap Off N.C. Legislature's Series of Power Grabs," *Facing South*, July 30, 2018, https://www.facingsouth.org/2018/07/ballot-changes-cap-nc-legislatures-series-power-grabs.

CHAPTER 24

Jim Morrill, "A Little-Noticed Ballot Change Could Have a Big Impact," *Charlotte Observer*, July 6, 2018, https://www.charlotteobserver.com/news/politics-government/election/article214381709.html.

Dallas Woodhouse (@DallasWoodhouse), "The North Carolina Republican Party @ncgop has made it clear that we see Anita Earls @Anita_Earls not only as a danger to the judiciary, but a danger to human life if she is elected. @MicheleNixNCGOP https://dangerousanitaearls.com," Twitter, June 13, 2018, https://twitter.com/DallasWoodhouse/status/1006920146118758401.

Mark Joseph Stern, "North Carolina Republicans' Latest Judicial Power Grab May Have Backfired Spectacularly," *Slate*, July 17, 2018, https://slate.com/news-and-politics/2018/07/north-carolina-republicans-plan-to-steal-a-state-supreme-court-seat-from-anita-earls-is-backfiring.html.

Interview, Earls.

Associated Press, "Late Candidacy Could Help Democrats Win NC Supreme Court Race," *Winston-Salem Journal*, July 5, 2018, https://journalnow.com/news/elections/late-candidacy-could-help-democrats-win-n-c-supreme-court-race/article_458f25af-7304-5210-b5d3-1fa3db655a8c.html.

Mark Barrett, "Hise Bill Would Hit Former Democrat Who Turned Republican in Supreme Court Race," *Asheville Citizen-Times*, July 25, 2018, https://www.citizen-times.com/story/news/local/2018/07/25/nc-legislators-pass-ralph-hise-bill-change-supreme-court-race/833945002/.

Melissa Boughton, "Judge Puts NCGA's Retroactive Change of Judicial Filing Rules on Hold for the Moment," *NC Policy Watch*, August 6, 2018, http://pulse.ncpolicywatch.org/2018/08/06/judge-puts-lawmakers-change-of-judicial-filing-rules-on-hold-for-the-moment/.

CHAPTER 25

Yeoman, "The North Carolina GOP is Trying Every Trick to Keep a Supreme Court Seat."

Melissa Boughton, "PW Exclusive: A Q&A with All Three NC Supreme Court Candidates," *NC Policy Watch*, July 9, 2018, http://www.ncpolicywatch.com/2018/07/09/pw-exclusive-a-qa-with-all-three-nc-supreme-court-candidates/.

Editorial, "For Supreme Court - Anita Earls," *WRAL*, November 2, 2018, https://www.wral.com/editorial-for-n-c-supreme-court-anita-earls/17963371/.

Editorial, "N.C. GOP Tries Again to Stack the Deck," *Virginian-Pilot*, August 2, 2018, https://www.pilotonline.com/opinion/article_c799a5a0-95c4-11e8-8aaf-7ff539e654b9.html.

Interview, Earls.

CHAPTER 26

"Democrat Anita Earls Declares Victory in NC Supreme Court Race," The News & Observer, YouTube, November 6, 2018, https://www.youtube.com/watch?v=f3NXw3PV5ng.

Billy Corriher, "The Diverging Fates of Two N.C. Lawyers who Battled over Voter Suppression," *Facing South*, December 6, 2018, https://www.facingsouth.org/2018/12/diverging-fates-two-nc-lawyers-who-battled-over-voter-suppression.

Community Success Initiative v. Moore, No. 19 CVS 15941 (N.C. Super. Ct. 2020), https://wwwcache.wral.com/asset/news/state/nccapitol/2020/09/04/19271163/community_success_v._moore_order_on_injunctive_relief-DMID1-5o2xb3qgn.pdf.

Travis Fain, "Judges Open N.C. Voting to Some Felons on Probation," *WRAL*, September 4, 2020, https://www.wral.com/judges-open-nc-voting-to-some-felons-on-probation/19270899/.

Jordan Wilkie, "NCSBE Works With DPS to Find North Carolina Residents Affected by Ruling," *Carolina Public Press*, September 11, 2020, https://carolinapublicpress.org/37700/restoring-vote-nc-felons-ruling/.

Billy Corriher, "N.C. Supreme Court Orders Hearings on Racial Bias Against Death Row Inmates," *The Supreme Courts*, June 5, 2020, https://thesupremecourts.org/2020/06/05/n-c-supreme-court-orders-hearing-on-racial-bias-against-death-row-inmate/.

North Carolina v. Ramseur, No. 388A10 (N.C. 2020).

North Carolina v. Hobbs, No. 263PA18 (N.C. 2020).

"2018 Turnout Demonstrates Youth Enthusiasm, Demographic Shifts," Democracy North Carolina, https://democracync.org/news/2018-turnout-demonstrates-youth-enthusiasm-demographic-shifts/.

Mark Barrett, "Proposed NC Amendments Shift Governor's Power on Judges, Elections Board," *Asheville Citizen Times*, November 2, 2018, https://www.citizen-times.com/story/news/local/2018/11/02/proposed-nc-amendments-shift-governor-power-judges-elections/1857244002/.

Billy Corriher, "The End of the N.C. Legislature's War on Judicial Independence?" *Facing South*, June 6, 2019, https://www.facingsouth.org/2019/06/end-nc-legislatures-war-judicial-independence.

Nick Martin, "The Lingering Ghost of the North Carolina GOP Supermajority," *Splinter*, November 16, 2018, https://splinternews.com/the-lingering-ghost-of-the-north-carolina-republican-su-1830347296.

Billy Corriher, "N.C. Voter Suppression Architects Prepare to Strike Again," *Facing South*, November 20, 2018, https://www.facingsouth.org/2018/11/nc-voter-suppression-architects-prepare-strike-again.

CHAPTER 27

Jessica Huseman, "N.C. Governor Loses Re-Election Bid, Attempts to Hold Power by Claiming Voter Fraud," *ProPublica*, November 30, 2016, https://www.propublica.org/article/pat-mccrory-re-election-bid-attempts-hold-power-claiming-voter-fraud.

Kareem Crayton, "Judge Rules Accusations of Voter Fraud Can Be Defamatory; Plaintiffs' Claims to Proceed to Trial," Southern Coalition for Social Justice, January 3, 2020, https://southerncoalition. org/judge-rules-accusations-of-voter-fraud-can-be-defamatory-plaintiffs-claims-to-proceed -to-trial/.

Complaint, *DeLuca v. Board of Elections*, No. 16-913, N.C. Super. Ct., November 21, 2016, https://www.nccivitas.org/wp-content/uploads/2016/11/CivitasFedFililng11_21.pdf.

Steve Harrison, "Bishop Wins Reelection in NC's 9th District," *WFAE*, November 4, 2020, https:// www.wfae.org/politics/2020-11-04/bishop-wins-reelection-in-ncs-9th-district.

Editorial, "Legislative Leadership Needs to Heed 'New Sheriff' in Town," *WRAL*, November 20, 2018, https://www.wral.com/editorial-legislative-leadership-needs-to-heed-new-sheriff-in-town/18008320/.

Herbert White, "NC Voters, Civil Rights Advocates Sue to Block Voter ID," *Charlotte Post*, December 23, 2018, http://www.thecharlottepost.com/news/2018/12/23/local-state/ nc-voters-civil-rights-advocates-sue-to-block-voter-id/.

Erika Williams, "4th Circuit Upholds North Carolina Voter ID Law," *Courthouse News Service*, December 2, 2020.

NAACP v. Raymond, No. 20-109 (4th Cir., Dec. 2, 2020), https://law.justia.com/cases/federal/ appellate-courts/ca4/20-1092/20-1092-2020-12-02.html.

Complaint, *Holmes v. Moore*, No. 18 CVS 15292, N.C Super. Ct., December 19, 2018, https:// southerncoalition.org/wp-content/uploads/2019/01/Holmes-v-Moore-Final.pdf.

Southern Coalition for Social Justice, "New North Carolina Voter ID Law Immediately Challenged by Voters," SCSJ press release, December 19, 2018, https://southerncoalition.org/ new-north-carolina-voter-id-law-immediately-challenged-voters/.

Melissa Boughton, "Wake County judge: Voter ID Challenge Can Move Forward in Courts," *NC Policy Watch*, March 14, 2019, http://pulse.ncpolicywatch.org/2019/03/14/ wake-county-judge-voter-id-challenge-can-move-forward-in-courts/.

Sen. Warren Daniel and Sen. Joyce Krawiec, "Statement on Voter ID Appeals Court Ruling," Senator Berger Press Shop press release, February 18, 2020, https://bergerpress.medium.com/ statement-on-voter-id-appeals-court-ruling-78810f6b0e96.

CHAPTER 28

Alex Amend, "From Eugenics to Voter ID Laws: Thomas Farr's Connections to the Pioneer Fund," *Southern Poverty Law Center*, December 4, 2017, https://www.splcenter.org/hatewatch/2017/12/04/ eugenics-voter-id-laws-thomas-farrs-connections-pioneer-fund.

Thomas Goldsmith, "Thomas Farr, Jesse Helms, and the Return of the Segregationists," *Indy Week*, January 3, 2018, https://indyweek.com/news/thomas-farr-jesse-helms-return-segregationists/.

Joe Patrice, "Asking About Brown v. Board Is 'Gutter Politics,' According To Senate Judiciary Official," *Above the Law*, May 10, 2018, https://abovethelaw.com/2018/05/asking-about -brown-v-board-is-gutter-politics-according-to-senate-judiciary-official/.

Melissa Boughton, "Trump Nominee Farr Could be Confirmed to Eastern District Judgeship by End of Year," *NC Policy Watch*, November 16, 2018, http://pulse.ncpolicywatch.org/2018/11/16/ trump-nominee-farr-could-be-confirmed-to-eastern-district-judgeship-by-end-of-year/.

William Barber (@RevDrBarber), "Tim Scott cast the deciding vote for cloture on the judicial nomination of Thomas Farr, who has promoted racist public policy for decades. This vote vs voting rights for African-Americans is what internalized racism & political delusion look like.," Twitter, November 28, 2018, https://twitter.com/RevDrBarber/status/1067915965113999360.

NAACP, "Watch Derrick Johnson speak out against Thomas Farr at the Demand Justice Rally on Capitol Hill," June 6, 2018, https://www.facebook.com/watch/live/?v=10155588844313947&ref=watch_permalink.

Meg Kinnard, "GOP Senator Sinks Trump Nominee, Lands in the Spotlight," *Associated Press*, November 30, 2018, https://apnews.com/article/5300e248d1734ef2b7e3a83897b7f616.

Thomas Kaplan, "White House Withdraws Appeals Court Nominee Who Deplored Multiculturalism," *New York times*, July 19, 2018, https://www.nytimes.com/2018/07/19/us/politics/trump-judge-senate-bounds.html.

Adam Serwer, "The Conscience of a Conservative," *The Atlantic*, December 3, 2018, https://www.theatlantic.com/ideas/archive/2018/12/tim-scotts-stand-against-voter-disenfranchisement/577132/.

Emma Dumain and Bryan Murphy, "Scott to Oppose Farr Nomination to Federal Bench in NC, Ending Chances of Confirmation," *McClatchy*, November 29, 2018, https://www.mcclatchydc.com/news/politics-government/congress/article222386255.html.

Tanasia Kenney, "Democrats Shame Sen. Tim Scott for Supporting Trump Nominee Who Supported Legislation to Hurt Black Voters," *Atlanta Black Star*, November 29, 2018, https://atlantablackstar.com/2018/11/29/democrats-shame-sen-tim-scott-for-supporting-trump-nominee-who-supported-legislation-to-hurt-black-voters/.

CHAPTER 29

Associated Press, "Republicans Pitch Keeping Court of Appeals at 15 Judges," *WFAE*, February 19, 2019, https://www.wfae.org/politics/2019-02-19/republicans-pitch-keeping-court-of-appeals-at-15-judges#stream/0.

Billy Corriher, "Lawsuit Targets Racially Gerrymandered N.C. Judicial Elections," *Facing South*, August 27, 2019, https://www.wfae.org/politics/2019-02-19/republicans-pitch-keeping-court-of-appeals-at-15-judges#stream/0.

Complaint, *Alexander v. Board of Elections*, 19 CVS ____, N.C. Super. Ct., https://www.facingsouth.org/sites/default/files/Complaint%20Final%20Version%20PDF.pdf.

Morrill, "Judges in Mecklenburg Judicial Districts Scrambling Days Before Election Filing."

David Daley, "The Secret Files of the Master of Modern Republican Gerrymandering," *The New Yorker*, September 6, 2019, https://www.newyorker.com/news/news-desk/the-secret-files-of-the-master-of-modern-republican-gerrymandering.

Billy Corriher, "N.C. Judges Asked to Speed Up Trial Over 'Racially Segregated' Judicial Elections," *Facing South*, November 21, 2019, https://www.facingsouth.org/2019/11/nc-judges-asked-speed-trial-over-racially-segregated-judicial-elections.

N.C. General Assembly, House, *An Act Amending the Campaign Finance Laws to Raise the Limit on Merchandise Sales for Political Parties and to Provide for At-Large Election of District Court Judges in Mecklenburg County*, SB 782, 2019 sess. https://www.ncleg.gov/BillLookUp/2019/S782.

CHAPTER 30

Plaintiff's Memorandum in Support of Motion for Temporary Restraining Order and Preliminary Injunction, *NAACP v. Moore*, No. CV 009806, August 6, 2018, https://www.coastalreview.org/wp-content/uploads/2018/08/Plaintiffs-Memorandum-in-Support-of-Motion-for-TRO-and-PI-August-6.pdf.

Lisa Worf, "Why Court Ruled N.C. GOP's Amendment Process Was Unconstitutional," *WFAE*, February 25, 2019, https://www.wfae.org/politics/2019-02-25/why-court-ruled-n-c-gops-amendment-process-was-unconstitutional.

Billy Corriher, "North Carolina's 'Usurper' Legislature Challenged on Amending Constitution," *Facing South*, August 14, 2018, https://www.facingsouth.org/2018/08/north-carolinas-usurper-legislature-challenged-amending-constitution.

Billy Corriher, "Can a Racially Gerrymandered Legislature Amend the N.C. Constitution?," *Facing South*, July 18, 2019, https://www.facingsouth.org/2019/07/can-racially-gerrymandered-legislature-amend-nc-constitution.

Sydney Trent, "A Black Voting Rights Activist Confronts the Ghosts of Racial Terror in North Carolina," *Washington Post*, October 29, 2020, https://www.washingtonpost.com/history/2020/10/29/wilmington-coup-massacre-election-trump/.

Billy Corriher, "A Blow to 'Usurper' Elected Officials in North Carolina," *Facing South*, March 12, 2019, https://www.facingsouth.org/2019/03/blow-usurper-elected-officials-north-carolina.

Billy Corriher, "Legal Fight Continues Over Amendments Passed by Gerrymandered N.C. Legislature," *Facing South*, September 16, 2020, https://www.facingsouth.org/2020/09/legal-fight-continues-over-amendments-passed-gerrymandered-nc-legislature.

NAACP v. Moore, No.COA19-384, September 15, 2020, https://appellate.nccourts.org/opinions/?c=2&pdf=38969.

CHAPTER 31

Rucho v. Common Cause, 139 S.Ct. 2484 (2019).

Tara Golshan and Ella Nilsen, "A North Carolina Court Just Threw Out Republicans' Gerrymandered State Legislature Map," *Vox*, September 3, 2019, https://www.vox.com/policy-and-politics/2019/9/3/20848087/north-carolina-court-republican-gerrymander-state-legislature-map.

Billy Corriher, "There's Still Hope to Stop Partisan Gerrymandering in North Carolina," *Facing South*, June 28, 2019, https://www.facingsouth.org/2019/06/theres-still-hope-stop-partisan-gerrymandering-north-carolina.

Melissa Boughton, "The Gerrymanderer's Daughter," *NC Policy Watch*, December 20, 2019, http://www.ncpolicywatch.com/2019/12/20/the-gerrymanderers-daughter/.

Erika Williams, "Expert Witness says Mapmaker Used Racial Data to Create North Carolina Voting Districts," *Courthouse News*, July 16, 2019, https://www.courthousenews.com/expert-witness-says-mapmaker-used-racial-data-to-create-n-c-voting-districts/.

Melissa Boughton, "Key Expert Witness on Day 2 of Testimony in Partisan Gerrymandering Trial," *NC Policy Watch*, July 17, 2019, http://pulse.ncpolicywatch.org/2019/07/17/key-expert-witness-on-day-2-of-testimony-in-partisan-gerrymandering-trial/.

Common Cause v. Lewis, No. 18 CVS 014001 (N.C.Sup.Ct. 2019), http://commoncause.org/north-carolina/wp-content/uploads/sites/22/2019/09/Common-Cause-v.-Lewis-trial-court-decision-9.3.19.pdf.

Billy Corriher, "When will North Carolina Get Fair Election Districts?," *Facing South*, September 11, 2019, https://www.facingsouth.org/2019/09/when-will-north-carolina-get-fair-election-districts.

Billy Corriher, "North Carolina may have fairer congressional districts by 2020," *Facing South*, October 10, 2019, https://www.facingsouth.org/2019/10/north-carolina-may-have-fairer-congressional-districts-2020.

Plaintiffs' Motion for a Preliminary Injunction, *Harper v. Lewis*, No. 19 CVS 012667, September 3, 2019, https://static1.squarespace.com/static/5beeefdbf407b4c074e45ec6/t/5d9273470ca873256 6705b2e/1569878859112/Harper+v.+Lewis+-+PI+Motion.pdf.

"The Full Transcript of ALEC's 'How to Survive Redistricting' Meeting," *Slate*, October 2, 2019, https://slate.com/news-and-politics/2019/10/full-transcript-alec-gerrymandering-summit.html.

Joseph Ax, "North Carolina's Congressional Map is Illegal Republican Gerrymander, Court Rules," *Reuters*, October 28, 2019, https://www.reuters.com/article/us-north-carolina-gerry-mandering/north-carolinas-congressional-map-is-illegal-republican-gerrymander-court-rules-idUSKBN1X805D.

Sam Wang, "North Carolina's New House Plan Still Has at Least Half the Partisan Skew of the Gerrymandered Map," *Princeton Election Consortium*, September 14, 2019, https://election.princeton.edu/2019/09/14/north-carolinas-new-house-plan-contains-over-half-as-much-partisanship-as-the-original-gerrymander/.

Miles Parks, "A Surprise Vote, Thrown Phone and Partisan 'Mistrust' Roil N.C. As Maps Are Redrawn," *WUNC*, September 16, 2019, https://www.npr.org/2019/09/16/760177030/a-surprise-vote-thrown-phone-and-partisan-mistrust-roil-n-c-as-maps-are-redrawn.

Melissa Boughton, "4th Circuit Denies Legislative Bid to Move Old Redistricting Case Out of State Court," *NC Policy Watch*, March 17, 2020, http://pulse.ncpolicywatch.org/2020/04/17/4th-circuit-denies-legislative-bid-to-move-old-redistricting-case-out-of-state-court/.

David Wasserman, "Rating Changes: Final North Carolina Map Boosts House Democrats," *The Cook Political Report*, December 6, 2019, https://cookpolitical.com/analysis/house/north-carolina-house/rating-changes-final-north-carolina-map-boosts-house-democrats.

Billy Corriher, "Redistricting Rulings Were Pivotal to Democrats' Control of Congress," *The Supreme Courts*, January 11, 2021, https://thesupremecourts.org/2021/01/11/redistricting-rulings-were-pivotal-to-democrats-control-of-congress/.

Michael Li (@mcpli), "A reminder that we almost certainly wouldn't be having this day but for court-ordered redraws of politically and racially gerrymandered US House maps in PA, NC, VA, and FL. #ImpeachmentDay #fairmaps," Twitter, January 13, 2021, https://twitter.com/mcpli/status/1349416827164766214?s=20.

CONCLUSION

Berman, "North Carolina's Moral Mondays."

Steve Harrison, "The Voting Rights Act Turns 55 Today. It's Still Fiercely Contested In North Carolina.," *WFAE*, August 6, 2020, https://www.wfae.org/politics/2020-08-06/the-voting -rights-act-turns-55-today-its-still-fiercely-contested-in-north-carolina.

EPILOGUE

Tom Perkins, "Courts Likely to Strike Down Republican Lame-Duck Power Grabs, Experts Say," *The Guardian*, December 11, 2018, https://www.theguardian.com/us-news/2018/dec/11/ republican-lame-duck-power-grabs-unconstitutional-experts-say.

Billy Corriher, "Wisconsin Supreme Court Limits Power of Democratic Governor," *The Supreme Courts*, July 12, 2020, https://thesupremecourts.org/2020/07/12/wisconsin -supreme-court-limits-power-of-democratic-governor/.

League of Women Voters of Pa. v. Commonwealth, 178 A.3d 737 (Pa. 2018).

Billy Corriher, Pennsylvania May Be the Next State to Gerrymander Judges," *The Supreme Courts*, January 6, 2020, https://thesupremecourts.org/2020/01/06/pennsylvania -may-be-the-next-state-to-gerrymander-judges/.

Kadida Kenner, "Should Pa. Elect Judges Based on Geography?," *Philadelphia Inquirer*, February 4, 2021, https://www.inquirer.com/opinion/commentary/appellate-court-elections -pennsylvania-judicial-gerrymandering-20210204.html.

Billy Corriher, "Court Packing? It's Already Happening at the State Level," *Governing*, September 30, 2020, https://www.governing.com/now/Court-Packing-Its-Already-Happening-at-the -State-Level.html.

Patrick Berry and Douglas Keith, "In 2018, a Spate of Partisan Attacks on State Courts," *Brennan Center for Justice*, December 18, 2018, https://www.brennancenter.org/our-work/ analysis-opinion/2018-spate-partisan-attacks-state-courts.

Billy Corriher, "5 Republican Governors Trying to Control Judicial Selection," *The Supreme Courts*, September 23, 2019, https://thesupremecourts.org/2019/09/23/5-republican -governors-trying-to-control-judicial-selection/.

Lucia Walinchus, "Push Continues to Change how State Selects Top Judges," *Tulsa World*, August 14, 2016, https://tulsaworld.com/news/local/crime-and-courts/oklahoma-watch-push-continues -to-change-how-state-selects-top-judges/article_89535a25-f19c-56af-9c31-db8981fd1718.html.

David Daley, "Arizona Republicans Make Sneaky Moves to Rig Gerrymandering," *Salon*, January 14, 2021, https://www.salon.com/2021/01/14/arizona-republicans-make-sneaky-moves-to-rig -redistricting-commission-before-any-lines-are-drawn/.

Billy Corriher, "Texas Considers Ending Judicial Elections as Democrats Gain Ground," *Facing South*, November 6, 2019, https://www.facingsouth.org/2019/11/texas-considers -ending-judicial-elections-democrats-gain-ground.

Emma Platoff, "Will Texas Finally End Partisan Judicial Elections?" *Texas Tribune*, July 15, 2019, https://www.texastribune.org/2019/07/15/texas-partisan-judicial-elections-reform-abbott-support/.

Douglas Keith, "Much Is at Stake in State Supreme Court Elections — Who's Trying to Influence Them?" *Brennan Center for Justice*, September 22, 2020, https://www.brennancenter.org/our-work/ analysis-opinion/much-stake-state-supreme-court-elections-whos-trying-influence-them.

ACKNOWLEDGMENTS

Thank you to my parents for all of their support and encouragement over the years. I'm grateful to the editors, Susan Edwards and Shana Murph. Susan's help was crucial, and I couldn't have done this without her.

Thank you to Dan Almasy for designing the cover and Catherine Williams for laying out the interior.

I was fortunate to have three jurists—Judge Kim Best, Justice Anita Earls, and former Judge Bob Hunter—speak with me for hours about the events in this book.

I would also like to thank Melissa Kromm and some of my colleagues at the Institute for Southern Studies: Chris Kromm, Sue Sturgis, and Ben Barber.

Made in the USA
Columbia, SC
31 May 2021